MIRACLE MINDED MEDIUM

THE PURPOSE AND POWER OF TALKING TO DEAD PEOPLE

BRENDA L. MCCREA

Difference Press

Washington, DC, USA

Cover Design: Jennifer Stimson

Editing: Cory Hott

Author Photo Credit: Brenda McCrea / Be In The Love Studios

CONTENTS

For my Ka.

THE ONE WITH SPIRIT
WHISPERS

"Unconditional love is simply love with no strings attached."

— ANONYMOUS

I t happened again, didn't it?

You just got home and realized it did, didn't you?

You look around and shake if off like that can't be. You blink a few times. This discovery is re-playing in the back of your mind. Did you just see your grandpa? You talk yourself out of it. Obviously, it's not grandpa. He died years ago.

No, you're overthinking it. (Scooby and Shaggy fill your head with a big scream, "Zoiks, it can't be!")

Then you realize you are not. Right? Maybe? No? Yes...?

Sound familiar?

You keep your mind moving, like putting together a puzzle, and you are collecting all these data pieces. You go about your day but tonight you'll dive deeper to figure out what is going on.

Later that same night, you're ready to go to sleep and you review your day. You're brushing your teeth. Out of the corner of your eye, you see the profile of grandpa and smell his cologne. Then you check on the kids to make sure they are sleeping and your child asks you who the man is standing beside you. The smell of the cologne pulls your focus to the left, exactly the same place your child is pointing.

Grandpa?

You tuck your child into bed and make your way back to your own. On the way there, a friend, Patty, pops into your mind. The next thing you know, you're calling her on your phone. Patty answers and is having the worst day in her life and is so grateful you called. You are there for your friend, reminding her she is loved. What Patty doesn't know is you meant to call to find out about pick-up time in the morning. By the time you end your call with Patty, you ask about the pick-up time. She told you she had sent a text message prior to the phone call. She knew you would forget the 9:00 a.m. pick-up.

You ask yourself – what did I just experience? This happens all the time.

You have been through this before. It has not slowed down. This experience increases every day. You feel what it must be like to live in the movie Groundhog Day. You understand that every time you go against your gut, your instinct, or you do not acknowledge this interaction, your life gets a little bit more difficult.

How about this – you eagerly wait for the mail to arrive because an important package is on its way. You take a deep breathe in and realize you will receive a letter from an old friend. You feel happy you will hear from your old friend yet feel a huge sense of dread that your package will be delayed. You ask yourself, "How did I come to that thought?" An investigation must be launched into your thinking and patterns. You take a breath. Those are two random thoughts about mail. Later in the day, you go to retrieve the mail and booooom – the letter from an old friend arrived. Also, you received USPS notification that your package is delayed – and you were right about both.

HINDBRAIN

Our hindbrain keeps communication flowing – our mind tells our body when you are in fight or flight response. Our eyes continually scan our environment to see what is pulling our focus or what seems "off." According to britan nica.com, "The hindbrain coordinates functions that are fundamental to survival." This scanning is a natural human response. Right now, you are understanding that you answered a call – it just happened to be from Spirit. The response from your answer is keeping you puzzled.

Being puzzled can get annoying. Charlie Brown's "good grief" stamps into your mind. You want to understand what is going on and why this keeps happening. You see what is happening in your environment on a daily basis. Yet, it happens in the same way daily.

You have a busy life. Your calendar is filled with life events you need to focus on and this new communication experience is happening. What is this? Why is this? You know when you don't listen to your gut, things go wrong. You don't have time to figure out what is going on. There are too many times it has resulted in making your life harder. If feels like an energy "game" you are a participant in and you didn't know when the game started. How do you go about it?

You have tried to ignore your random thoughts. You talk yourself out of understanding that a loved one from heaven is speaking to you or appearing in front of you. Why you? But really, why not you? Sometimes you understand everything in your connection and other times, nothing makes sense. A guide book is needed.

It's time to address this. Now.

(RE)CALL

Someone is speaking to you. You answered the call. There is a frustration that washes over you. There is someone there who has your attention but the conversation flow seems to be under construction. You recall the long list of where, when, what happened, and to whom. It all seems scrambled. Having these experiences that logic does not have a part in can be overwhelming. Your faith in Spirit is strong, and you have asked for help, but you don't think they picked up your prayer yet.

I understand you. I've been there way too many times to recall. The confusion just overtakes you but your curiosity creates action to dig deeper into communicating with grandpa or others. Why do you see what you see? Why do you feel what you feel? Why do random thoughts, places, things, situations, and dead people pop into your head?

Shhh... don't tell anyone just yet but – lean in a little bit – this is huge. Oh, I'm so thrilled to share this with you. All these experiences you have are not random. They are specifically designed for you. In this time and space, you are right where you are supposed to be – on a new, beautiful journey, communicating in an entirely new form.

What is Willis talking about here? New form of communication with whom?

These random experiences are the key indicators that Spirit (while in this book, when referring to Spirit, it is also in reference to God and God's love) is communicating with you. You answered Spirit's call. Spirit knows you are ready to help those you encounter grow in love.

Our hindbrain regulates our brain for survival by telling our body to be a in fight or a flight response. Our gut feelings are another way to receive information about our environment. This new form of communication with Spirit starts with what you know and trust. You know what a gut feeling is and you trust it.

STOP THE CAR

My friend, Riley, was loving motherhood. Riley and her husband had a beautiful daughter named Olivia. She wanted help listening to her gut feeling. "I know you help your clients with this all the time. Will you work with me?" Riley asked. She kept having this gut feeling that she needed to update her speaking pattern with her daughter Olivia, who is three years old.

We got to work. Riley told me about her grandmother who was extremely prideful about communicating well. Riley giggled to herself because her mother would describe how her grandmother would make a certain sound when she sighed. It sounded like a low whistle through some trees.

Riley encouraged conversations with Olivia. Most importantly, she emphasized listening, as well as you could to a three-year-old. She thought, "What would my grandmother think about this?" Motherhood is good listening.

It takes time and practice to trust listening to your gut feelings. When you do, you will see and feel different about your gut feelings. This isn't something that is perfect overnight.

A few weeks later, Riley and Olivia were meeting me

for lunch across town. Riley and Olivia had two more streets to get to the restaurant. Riley passed their favorite grocery store and Olivia waved.

They were one stop away from the restaurant. Riley was stopped at a stop light and was first in line to proceed forward. She heard a scream.

Olivia screamed as loud as she could in a low whistle tone – "Stop car!"

Time slowed in that instant.

All Riley could hear was Olivia's conviction in her voice. This was not the normal sound Olivia made. This was not the vibrato she used when she wailed for cookies and does not get them. Riley went in her mind and realized I need to listen to my gut and child.

Riley immediately stopped the car. Olivia released this low sounding whistle that went through the trees. She immediately thought of her grandmother and her sigh. Riley looked in the rear-view mirror and Olivia was all by herself. How did Olivia make large sound?

Riley looked straight ahead and a large blue truck ran the red light. Listening to Olivia, Riley had stopped the car. It saved their lives.

Riley said, "Right before I put Olivia in the car seat, I told myself to listen to my gut feelings, listen to my child – all will be okay." She smelled her grandmother's perfume and thought, "How interesting," and kept going while smiling.

Riley never used to listen to her gut feelings. She used to rationalize away the experience instead.

It takes time to understand and train yourself to trust your gut. Before I did, I was so annoyed at myself and I had a daily reminder of "This is what happens when you don't listen to yourself," or "Listen to your gut," or "Listen to the message." Just listen.

GO AGAINST YOUR GUT FEELING

My husband and I just moved into our new home. We made huge updates to the home. Painting was the first on the agenda. We called a friend who would help with interior color themes. It was perfect.

We had beautiful sky lights in the master bedroom. The sun filled every corner of the room. It was like our sunburst. The last room would be the bedroom.

I was sorting the painting supplies and paint colors and put enough tape in all the places we needed. I was down stairs and I would see a quick snap shot of the sky light in the master bedroom with paint on it. Then I just would keep moving as I had a lot of painting to complete.

This would happen over and over. I'm in the kitchen painting. Quick snap shot of the sky light with paint on it.

Two days later we were in the bedroom. We were happy with the blue color of the bedroom. It turned out better and brighter with the sky light so bright. We were happy.

My husband noticed there was one side of the sky light that needed another coat of paint. I looked up and watched him get on the ladder and complete our painting. I thought to myself, "Tell him to use his dominant hand because he may lose his balance and paint may go everywhere like the sky light." I didn't say anything. Not one word to my husband to be careful. I knew he knew what he was doing.

The next minute my husband was on the ladder with the paint brush in the wrong hand. He lost his balance and there was a beautiful paint mark on the sky light. It was the exact quick snap shot I had seen over and over for the last few days.

I told my husband and we both said that this was one

painting story. That paint mark was a daily reminder of what not to do.

SIGNS OF LOVE

You're out to run some errands and as you go to the car, you look back because you are for sure smelling some good perfume. It takes you back to when you were five years old and Aunty Eloise pinched your cheeks and smelled of peaches. You remembered how slow Aunty Eloise drove and then giggled. You brush it off as if someone must have the same perfume near you but you are the only one in the parking lot.

You continue driving and turn on the radio and Aunty Eloise's favorite song plays. You hear in your head Aunty Eloise tell you, "You drive too fast."

You're ready to get your coffee at your favorite place and the barista calls out the name of your friend who just passed for your coffee.

Or that one time, you went to the festival in town and the crowd was big and the lines were long. You turn to your right and do a double take and look because you think you saw your childhood dog at the park and he's not there.

You reach for your phone, and the person you want to call is already calling you. It happens more times than not.

Out for a walk and out of the corner of your eye, you notice something moved yet you are alone. While on a walk, the same coin shows up in the bathroom, carport, driveway, washing machine, and your kitchen counter. Then you look at the year and feel nostalgia.

The electricity in your house flickers, and light bulbs burn out at a faster rate. You also noticed the lights dancing in the house. On and off the radio turns while playing Aunt Simone's favorite song – and the radio is not plugged in.

You receive smart phones notifications that you never set up on your phone. Or the calendar notification goes off and no calendar entry has been made but you realize, after noticing the date, that it's your friend's birthday. The lost voicemail from a loved one that you deleted populates for a second time in your voicemail box as if it is new.

Your name being called sounds out in a public place. You thought you heard your Grandpa's voice call your name but you don't see him. How would you see him? He died years ago.

Nature has always been in constant communication with us. The interaction with animals, the landscape, and the elements speaks louder than words. The clouds create pictures in the sky that fill your heart with love because the cloud formation reminds you of your childhood cat.

You play music after coming home from a long day of living life hard. You just want to feel supported and loved; your favorite song by the Mowglis, "San Francisco" (DJ Pumpkin Remix) plays and your whole day washes away with love.

You feel a sudden urge to take action – as though you are watching your body slow – and your thoughts are highly focused. You take action and pick up your phone to call someone. You unlock your phone and your friend is already saying hello. Neither one of you called each other – it just happened.

SYNCHRONISTIC EVENTS: JACK JOHNSON CONCERT TICKETS

Speaking of synchronistic events, Carl Jung defines them as, "Synchronic meaningful coincidence." The synchronistic events are not points that relate but the events are most definingly connected in a particular way.

My friend Bree was visiting for an overnight stay. We have been friends since we were two years old. We met in pre-school. We tried to get Jack Johnson concert tickets but it was sold out.

My husband went to work while Bree and I had a fun day together. Little did we know, at my husband's work there was a raffle for three fun prizes: Steak House gift card, baseball Angels tickets, and Jack Johnson concert tickets.

My husband won the steak house prize. Jace won baseball tickets but wanted the steak house prize because he wanted to eat there forever and he wanted to take his parents. So, they switched tickets. My husband had the baseball tickets.

Ben won the Jack Johnson tickets but wanted the Angel's tickets because he loves the Angels more than Jack Johnson. They switched.

My husband dropped off the Jack Johnson tickets for us to attend the show. He had to tell us how it all transpired. Then my husband said to me, when I left this morning, you said, "Thanks for getting us the tickets." He told me, "I thought you were confused but you were right – I got the concert tickets."

Bree and I had the best time at the concert. It was meant to be and I was grateful to all who were involved because that experience with Bree is priceless. What my husband did was extraordinary and synchronized it all to be.

SPIRIT IS TALKING

The new way of communication you have been experiencing has a label called "medium." You hold the space and energy in between the Spirit world and the earth plane. You are the medium who connects the communication. The National Spiritualist Associations of Churches defines "A Spirit Medium is one whose organism is sensitive to vibrations from the Spirit World, and through whose instrumentality, intelligences in that world are able to convey messages and produce the phenomena of Spiritualism." Our lives are so busy already – to add a new communication form seems impossible. Yet Spirit will keep communicating with you until you respond.

I want you to be as prepared as you can be to speak with Spirit. Building your communication is a bit strange at first but exercising this communication muscle will be worth it. These events are happening to you for a reason. You are ready to unlock your style of communication with Spirit. Welcome to your gifts from Spirit. Welcome to Spirit mediumship.

There are two different types of mediums – mental and physical, and you may be both. For the purpose of this book, we will focus on mental mediumship which encompasses Spirit communication. A physical medium is defined with some attributes of healing, automatic writing, matter materialization, and levitation. A mental medium is defined as clairvoyance – seeing the soul, clairaudience – hearing the soul, and clairsentience – sensing the soul.

When mastering the gift of clairvoyance, Spirit will often help you comprehend what you are seeing before you. Things will be slowed down and you will be able to comprehend your environment visually in a new way. You see Spirit in physical form. You receive symbols from

Spirit to help you both connect. This is the space where you get to use your creativity and define symbols for Spirit communication. A lot of mediums have a red balloon as a symbol as a celebration event coming into their loved one's life. If you don't like the color red or a balloon, you can change it with Spirit. Spirit wants you to have your set of symbols so you understand what is being communicated.

One of my favorite aunts would make her presence known by giving me this wonderful fish dish she would make. It was a salty smelly fish. I hated the smell. I asked if we can change that smell into her favorite flower smell instead. It worked.

Experiencing clairaudience is a real treat because you get to hear what the Spirit sounded like when they were in physical form on earth. There are so many Spirits ready to speak to you and it doesn't take a lot of energy for Spirit to manifest audio. Let the Spirit chatting begin.

The clairsentience of mediumship is sensing the soul. This is complex. Think about your best friend right now. You have a picture of them in your head right now. Everything about them that you can think of is your internal blueprint of them. When Spirit uses clairsentience, this what they do – you can't see your friend but you can hear their voice in your head and visualize them or get impressions. Spirit uses impression to give you information on the loved ones.

You are on your way to understanding your senses. Take some time to think about more Spirit instances; I know there is more to communication to discover with you.

2

THE ONE WITH UNDERSTANDING HOW SPIRIT IS

"Law of Attraction – Everything is energy and that's all there is to it. Match the frequency of the reality you want and you cannot help but get that reality. It can be no other way. This is not philosophy. This is physics."

— ALBERT EINSTEIN

L egendary comedian Norm Macdonald said it best, "I come from a long line of dead people."

I thought I was like everyone else. I thought everyone had waffles at breakfast with their dead grandpa. I thought I would grow up, get a job, get married, own dogs – that whole story. What I didn't realize is that we are all different people. Different people experience different things but not everybody speaks to Spirit or their dead grandpa at breakfast. What I also didn't realize is that grandpa died a year before I was born. He didn't look dead to me. He looked just like my gram...alive.

He was familiar to me. Familiar like when you know

that someone loves you. I know he loved me. I didn't know his name. We didn't speak. Just head nods. I smiled at him and then watched him disappear through the wall.

It wasn't until I was around eleven years old when I fully realized that dead people see me.

You see, this life experience is an everyday occurrence for me. I don't know what life is like in any other way. I thought everyone had the same shared experiences, it was just with their family. I would see how we as humans are all connected together so it made sense, we would all have a shared experience. It never occurred to talk about it to my friends. I didn't talk about it because we went to church and you never discussed your relationship with Spirit to anyone else. You showed people what your relationship with Spirit was by doing this: you went to church and prayed.

I thought to myself, I have been educated in the church to keep talking to Spirit. Pray daily. Pray for others. Pray for better situations. Pray for love and faith and to be strong. Father Byron told me to talk to Spirit every day. Talk to Spirit for other people. Talk to Spirit for myself. Say prayer for myself then prayer for others. I felt good about my relationship with Spirit. Spirit was cool and I felt the love. Mother Mary felt wonderful. Every time I prayed, the energy of love bathed me. I felt better.

I never felt right if I didn't start and end my day with prayer. I felt off. The full circle of prayer settled well within my heart and love of Spirit. My Gram insisted I pray as much as I could daily. My Gram prayed so much I thought she taught the Pope how to pray. The prayers were so long too.

IT BEGINS

I remember being small. I remember looking out and being in a crib. I remember standing in a crib. One time, I wanted to climb out and there was this man there and he just was filled with love and kindness. His hair was white as light shining through tree in a forest. I remember he had a great smile and it made his nose look bigger. Then he rolled his eyes and made funny faces. Then he just stared directly into my eyes as if he wanted me to watch him. I did and he traveled right through the wall toward the end of the house.

I called him my buddy. Our relationship grew and we played more and more but he would just pop in and say hi. Everywhere I went, he was there. I thought everyone in the family knew him yet no one talked to him. It wasn't until I was eleven years old when I realized he was in Spirit.

My buddy and I played and at this picnic we were about to talk, and someone sat right on top of my buddy and he disappeared right before my eyes. Then I freaked out. No one cared that he vanished. I thought, "Oh, everyone knows that he can do that." I never mentioned it because I thought everyone experienced what I had. I saw less and less of him as I got older.

I found in my diary every entry was about the dreams I had. Patrick is going to trip me tomorrow on the playground stay away from him. Next diary entry. Patrick tripped me on the playground and I tried to stay away and it happened anyway.

Another dream would be, I ask my Gram about going to her friend's house that she hasn't seen in years because they miss her. My Gram would call and her friend would tell her that, the first thing when they connected. The next time I would see my Gram I shared my dream and she did exactly what happened in my dream. She got re-connected with her friend.

In my prayers, I asked Spirit for help. Help to under-stand the world. Help me understand myself and these experiences of this world. Help me Spirit, through your love and guidance.

I thought everyone knew dead people saw them. I never had a fear because I knew I was protected because I have a relationship with Spirit. I believed in Spirit's love and that love would give me everything I needed to live this life, teaching and receiving love. Little did I know praying as much as I did also set me up to return to the other side more than a few times in my life.

MY MISSION FROM SPIRIT

Spirit gave me my mission. I pushed and pulled. I took a test that told you what you are to be when you grow up and mine came back inconclusive. I don't think they had Spirit medium as a career path.

The first time was brief and I was under the age of four years old. I don't have much about the distinctive details about what happened on the physical plane. I found that out much later when Gram told me.

Gram and I were playing and I was ready for a full day of fun. First, she handed me candy and I went to run. As I was running, the big fat piece of hard candy was in my lungs. I was choking. I have no memory of what happened on earth but in heaven, it was fantastic.

There is so much to share with you but first I need to tell you what happened to my physical body. I swallowed the hard candy and choked. My face turned blue and Gram said I kept coughing. My face turned bluer. I wasn't able to cough it out.

Then next thing I was turned upside down in hopes gravity would do its thing and free my lungs from this delicious piece of candy that my lungs didn't like. I was hit on the back in hopes of it falling out. (Please follow registered CPR protocol – do not follow this.) It did.

Gram said, I gasped for air and felt weird and looked around wondering what happened to all the kids I met in that other big room.

The next day, I was coloring in my coloring book and I asked Gram where that room was with all the kids and where did the kids go? I called out to them and couldn't find them anywhere. She asked me to tell her about it.

I explained, she gave me the hard candy and I went outside to play and then I was not outside I was in this huge room where you couldn't see the end of the walls. There were all kinds of kids there and they were floating around in well-formed lines. They all looked like they were in line for a ride or something. Everywhere I turned all these beautiful, gorgeous souls forming all these perfect lines.

Then this kind man said, "Hi, my name is Gabriel. You look lost." I was ready to say something and he said, "We can talk more in your prayers." There were sparkles everywhere. I felt in that moment I would talk to him again. Then I was in a new location – Gram's lap.

Years later, I understood that was the first time I saw heaven.

I remember retelling this story to my Gram every day. She told me that it was a special story. One that Jesus wrote especially for me and not to share it because it was private. I only spoke about it with her.

It would be another twelve years before I saw that room again in heaven. I never planned on it but there I was again. I was in a room, full of commotion and souls flying everywhere – but I didn't see Gabriel this time. I saw my buddy – my buddy who I would play with. I didn't know his name but I knew he was my buddy. I saw his profile and I could hear him speaking to me in my head. He had no body. He had head and shoulders – all normal features – but dissolved into black, as white, small sparkles. I tried to look at myself and didn't recognize myself.

All the colors were exaggerated, like the color pink. There were all the colors of pink that were ever thought of in the universe. Everything seemed to be full of love. There was peace. Everything you needed was right there and in pink.

You didn't have to breathe. Oh … the fact that you didn't have to breathe was so refreshing. I was so happy about that. The harshness of breathing I hated. I could do a back flip not breathing. Oh, I love it here now with no breathing.

I leaned left into my buddy and he said, "You have to go back to your body." I said, "No thanks. I'll stay here with you." This back and forth happened two more times.

I eventually went back into my body. I grasped for air. I was in a panic, not understanding what happened to my body or where I was. Then I remembered being given a shot in the arm.

Then I would be back up in the heaven's room with my buddy. I said, the second time. "Okay, I did what you asked I went back in my body. You are welcome." "Now what are we doing here," he said. "This time you have to stay in your body." I said, "Why?"

"There are several different reasons but the main ones

are you have more work to do on earth." I was not picking up what he was laying down. I thought for sure I needed to call Willis because I had no idea what he was talking about. By this time, I realized he was my Grandpa Bill, my gram's husband, and my buddy from when I was little.

I told him it was a bit silly he didn't tell me he was my grandpa before. We giggled and he said, "You didn't know what that word was." That made sense to me.

Grandpa Bill said to me. "What about Gram? What about Sean? They need you." I felt like I was sliding down a Fibonacci spiral telling my grandpa that wasn't fair to bring them up. I knew I was in my Fibonacci spiral back to my body.

Sure enough, I was back in my body.

BODY CHECK

Before I went back inside my body, I toured my environment before completely returning. I saw myself and didn't recognize myself at all. To see myself in 3D, I was not prepared for. The only part of myself that I recognized was my heart and the kind of love I share in my uniqueness. That is how I knew it was me.

I saw others gathered around me and took note of their conversations. The colors I witnessed were amazing. Like the pink color, there were multiple shades in every color within each color. The movie with Robin Williams, *What Dreams May Come*, is the closest example of how the other side looked to me.

I didn't see any tunnel with light at the end of it. I didn't see a pearly gate. I didn't see a bridge. What I did see was a bright light but that was already in the room. I saw Gabriel talking to his friends. He introduced me to his friend

Michael. We exchanged greetings. I had a strong knowing that I'd known these two souls for years. If I reflected on my life, I don't recall a time where I didn't feel Gabriel and Michael's love. Their love has been a constant in my life. Then I was back in my body.

THREE'S A CHARM

In my late twenties, I had been sick for a while. I wasn't sure what was going on. I had several health issues from the car accident and was heavily medicated. I had two medications which caused allergy issues and bleeding.

I went back in heaven's room with Gabriel then I was back at home. I was lying in bed not feeling well. I looked at my bedroom door and Grandpa Bill was standing at the door. He said to me, "If you don't get up right now and tell Sean, this will be your last death. You need the ER now. Do you want Sean to come home to you dead?"

I texted my husband, Sean, and said there is something wrong. "911 drugs too strong." I was rushed to the ER. I had two issues. First, I had an allergic reaction to pain medications; second, I had a bacterial infection. I was given the proper medication and healed. I would not have made it if Grandpa didn't show up.

FUN PART

You see the thing is, I never left the bedroom when Grandpa Bill told me to tell Sean I needed the ER. My phone was in the kitchen which was at the other end of the house. When my husband got home, I was in my bed. I never got up physically and texted my husband. Someone did. Grandpa? Spirit? He got the text.

I know my Grandpa Bill along with the Holy Spirit

texted my husband. I was sick. I was unconscious. I needed a miracle and the Holy Spirit granted me one.

Of all my death experiences, it never felt like dying was an end – just continuing from the other side. It gave me the understanding that we are all connected and prayer is your tool for concentrated, quality communication. Daily prayer is the key that unlocks your relationship with Spirit.

I pushed Spirit away so many times and the communication would just come back stronger. Or my interaction with someone would change the course of their life – but for me that was a five minute meeting. Spirit was speaking through me. I was listening to and trying to be the best message operator to relay Spirit's message to myself and to those around me.

NOT EVERYONE SEES AS YOU DO

I soon realized that not everyone speaks to the departed. Dead people see me and what do I do now? Every time I would push it away, the experience would pull harder at my heart. Spirit would show me, "See how you helped that person become happy?" Then I thought, "Well, through Spirit, I made this person happy. Through Spirit and Spirit's love this person is happy." I never realized I was the person making the connection. I was the message operator. Delivering Spirit's message to those in need would inspire action to see their life's path and how loved they are by Spirit. Spirit gave me the mission to love unconditionally and to be of service.

What was the truth for my life's plan? I thought, "Father Byron likes me. I'm sure the Pope is going to love me. Maybe I should check in with them in case Spirit contacted them regarding my life." I'm fun and full of love. I go to church and I don't remember a day I wasn't praying to Spirit or asking Him for help in some way, shape, or form.

I felt like I was in *The Blues Brothers* movie. I was on a "Mission from God." I was attracted to creating love and sharing it. Knowing that Spirit picked me and gave me – day after day – reasons for yes. Yes, you are experiencing the earth plane. Yes, you are experiencing the heavenly plane as well. Yes, you are able to read energy and do it well.

I had to speak to Father. Yes, Father Byron said, "God wants you to be of service and be love." I said yeah, "I see him all the time and I want to make sure I was doing his work according to his love. I wanted to check in with you, Father." He laughed when I suggested we call the Pope. He told me that I was overthinking and to just be a kid – God doesn't work like that. I said, "Through love? I've been listening to you tell us that for years at church."

I believed Father Byron and let it go. Okay Spirit, I checked and I'm not supposed to do this work for you. God or Spirit had a different plan than Father Byron told me. It didn't settle well with the direction from Father. I did what I was told, I stopped listening, I stopped seeing, I stopped praying, and I stopped loving. It was the worst human experience and I didn't feel great. The world seemed flat to me: no life, no color, no sparkle of life at all. No person, place, or thing was fun. It was one dimensional.

OH GOD THE MOVIE

George Burns made an *Oh God II* movie and it replayed on TV for years. I remember in the movie, there was a statement that said, "Think God." In that moment, I remembered how I had stopped praying to Spirit. I remembered how I was confident when I had a strong relationship with

Spirit. I knew how to talk; Spirit was my friend. I didn't feel like he was my friend after speaking to Father.

I made the commitment and started praying again. It wasn't long after that I would interact with people and I would share Spirit's message for them through his love.

I would sit down with people and relay the message from Spirit which gave them advice to move forward in their life with love. I was fourteen years old and shopping at Kmart. I told a Kmart employee how to have a better relationship with her husband. I didn't know her or anything about a marriage or a relationship. The woman looked me in the eyes and thanked me for it. She said she needed to hear that wisdom to pull her out of the depression she was in. I was happy for her. I couldn't wait to see her again when I went shopping there. It happened, the next time I saw her she was happy and having a baby with husband. Everything worked out and Spirit's message was the love she needed.

ACTION BEFORE YOU KNOW WHY

There are times where I would make purchases before I knew why I was making them. I didn't have a lot of money growing up so buying extra things and not knowing why was strange for me. I would pray and ask for guidance. I felt the presence of Spirit and let my fear go. One time, I bought a condolence card and I didn't know anyone that died. When I got to my Gram's house, she told me her best friend had died. I consoled her and asked what can I do for her or her friend. Gram asked if I had a sympathy card in my pocket to send to her daughter. Yes, I just bought one. Gram told me the card I purchased was the same one she had bought and accidentally thrown it out. Spirit gave me the message someone needed this card and now I understand it is you. We mailed the card that day.

Praying to Spirit and building that relationship again was tough, but it was necessary for me to move forward and understand how to communicate with Spirit and understand how to set myself up for receiving.

I take this gift from Spirit seriously. It has filled me with the most beautiful love and has knocked me down to my knees. If I meet you in person, I'm not going to come up to you and say Uncle Jon says hi. No. No. No. No. I will tell you that if Spirit wants me to communicate a message from your loved one to you, there are several things that need to happen first.

You are here reading my book, so I don't want you to take the long road that hurt and scared me. That was never Spirit's plan. That was my fear that took over. I am in communion with Spirit and Spirit's love, which I do all actions through. I know who I am in this relationship and who Spirit is. Why and how He lets love flow through me to be of service to myself and to others. It humbles me.

When I put others before my Spirit relationship, chaos reigned over my life. Understand that there are spiritual policies to abide by. They are in place so you and others are safe and to guide you in Spirit's love. If the loved ones I communicate with do not follow the same policies, I explain my zero-tolerance policy. If these boundaries are not healthy, life is not good.

Having been to the other side and back several times, you get an insight into the other side. There are so many souls interacting in this universe. Keeping your life interpretation simple, judgment-free, joyful, and with gratitude has helped me understand why the human experience is so precious. We are so new to the world. Animals have instincts of all their behaviors and we have fight or flight. We don't even know what to eat when we are a baby.

Often times, I will give a message or share a vision I have had for someone and they ask, "I'm curious. How do you have that knowing? How do you receive your information?"

These are great questions. I meditate and pray daily. I have practiced this from the early stages in life and wanted a cultivated relationship with Spirit. My relationship history with Spirit is so strong that my knowing his message is clear. The knowing is you totally accepting Spirit and His plan so that you step aside in your mind to receive the full message. You state the full message without altering it and then realize you question yourself. Where did that come from? I wasn't thinking that. Oh yeah, Spirit was and He sent the message to me through the love vibration.

I know that is off-putting right now. You are taking the time to build a closer relationship with Spirit to love, to share love, and to be love. To be in that love is humbling. It is sacred. It is precious. No two experiences are the same. Each is unique and leaves a love impression on my soul.

My experiences here and on the other side have reaffirmed that we are all in this life together. We are all connected. Why not learn how to have a deeper, richer, quality filled life communicating with Spirit or Spirit or Source or Universal Love? Spirit understands that different people are different. Therefore, so are labels. The meaning behind the label does not change. The action behind the label name does not change and that is love. Everything we filled our minds with – why we can't – and is nonsense we made up because it is easier than having a relationship with Spirit.

You already have established your relationship with

Spirit. You don't have to spend half your life to figure this out. I'll provide you with the keys to start a deeper relationship with Spirit so you may help yourself to help others. Time to broaden your communication with Spirit. Let's get started.

3

THE ONE WITH SPIRIT
DECODING

"Birth in the physical is death in the spiritual. Death in the physical is birth in the spiritual."

— EDGAR CAYCE

Spirit is communicating with you daily. When you don't listen to your gut or Spirit, your life is harder. More steps need to be taken to get back on track. You can't turn back now because this resonates with you. Everything you read feels like you need the next step.

Sometimes you understand what to do. Sometimes you think you listened well and nothing happened. Please know you have not been trained on how to key in on this one of a kind communication. This energy shift happened. You have opened up to Spirit in a new way and have been introduced to this new gift. Let's see what medium skills Spirit has gifted you.

You prayed for help and this book is your answer.

WHISPERS

Spirit communication is coming from a place of love and service, so it will be set up for the best experience with Spirit. First, you hear the whispers of Spirit communication and understand you are a medium.

Like learning anything new, when Spirit starts to whisper, collecting data of your experiences is what you need. This is what Spirit gave you: the gift of mediumship. Time to learn about the different types of mediums and what it takes to have your mind, body, and soul prepared to communicate with Spirit.

SENSES

The sensory ignition of what feels like is what it means to communicate with Spirit. The Mind Body Reaction Faction is when your sense of reality is altered because you are communicating with energy in a whole new way. You are fully conscious, but see forms of energy clearer than prior experiences. One example is when I saw my grandpa the first time versus the last time.

When you are about to leave the house, you hear Grandma tell you the curling iron is left on in the bathroom. Yes, it sure is when you check it. You used your sense of hearing. Spirit will tap into all your senses to get you the message the easiest way. That means the physical senses of sight, sound, smell, taste, and touch. There are also soul senses of intuition, peace, foresight, trust, and love. The physical and soul senses all go together, and you will add more as time goes by.

Spirit will use your senses to relate to your environment to get the message to you with the most clarity. There are several different ways to communicate and connect with Spirit. Sometimes it's difficult to make that connection first.

Just like learning anything new, the more you work with Spirit, the easier the connection and messages will be. Give yourself space and time to understand and process this new journey. This journey is what you put into it. Let's make this fun and turn the page and get started.

SEVEN KEYS TO CONNECT TO SPIRIT

Along with Spirit, I've created Seven Spirit Communication Keys to initiate the flow of energy between you and Spirit. To receive the most, the best way is to follow these keys. A repetitive action with Spirit is a sure way to establish a call to Spirit. Understanding how to use these seven keys will guide you and keep you safe.

The Seven Spirit Communication Keys

1. Key | Spirit's Love
2. Key | Intention
3. Key | Logic
4. Key | Dreams
5. Key | Life Stories
6. Key | Psychic
7. Key | Be in the Love

It seems like a lot of keys to learn. They are easy and they are just the beginning. You will add more as time goes on, as you grow and as Spirit has your guides grow. Your mind and body have started educating yourself already.

MIND AND BODY CONNECTION

The mind and body connection is important. If your mind and body are not healthy, Spirit will not be able to connect with you for the clearest message. We need to keep hydrated as this takes a lot of water from our bodies. Our minds need to be primed to connect. Meditation will be our mind's set up for Spirit communications.

The mind and body connection also helps with understanding the physical messages from Spirit. For example, if the loved one from the other side had migraines, you may feel in your head what it is like to feel the migraines they had experienced. You understand that you yourself did not have this physical symptom – this is a message from Spirit.

Knowing what your body is telling you is key at all times. You need to know your body and its aches and pains. Also, you need to know where you do not have aches and pains. For the longest time it was hard for me, but taking yoga classes has assisted me with this and it has paid off.

SPIRIT PATTERNS

We are all human and going through life together right here and right now. Spirit will give you a series of patterns to connect with. For example, when I see a loved one and they walk into my vision from the left or the right I will know what side of the family they are from. Spirit repeating this pattern over several times helped me understand this detail.

It works both ways. You may set up a pattern with Spirit. The keys are your first patterns to start with Spirit. As you further your experiences with Spirit, patterns will be cultivated on a deeper level and more intricate.

BE OF SERVICE USING GIFTS

Spirit asking you to be of service is a lot and you are ready. How do I know? You are already connecting and growing with Spirit Communication. How will you have a check and balance for this? This is why this book is here for your reference. After establishing the type of medium you are, connecting with other mediums is the best way to grow your gifts. This will allow you to be of service to Spirit in a safe way. Other mediums were just like you starting.

As you have more and more experiences with Spirit, the language you both have is special and unique and it grows. It grows fast. Sometimes it will be difficult to keep track. You will remember you are being of service and growing your connection is important.

Every day, we have new life experiences. These new life experiences are ways to grow our communication with Spirit. You will understand further how to interpret that. Spirit will communicate in real time what is happening to get your attention if you are missing the call to be of service.

There will be days when you just can't be of service to Spirit. Tell them you need the day off. They understand. I state a prayer and connect and let them know I'm safe – just need the day off. Boundaries are a must when being of service to Spirit.

ACCEPT IT OR LET IT GO

You have decided to be of service after knowing what happens when you go against your gut – your life gets messy. It makes sense to want an easier life. When we get an easier life, we sometimes take the harder path because we don't think we deserve it. You deserve these gifts from

Spirit. Spirit would not give them to you if you were not ready. Plus, I would not have written this book if it wasn't for the Author Incubator. I prayed to Spirit for help and here I am and you are reading my book. Thank you, Spirit and AI team.

There will be a time for you to decide to move forward, and fully accept your gifts or let the gifts go. Every action has a pro and con. Yes, this is a wonderful gift to bring a message from loved ones on the other side to those on earthly plane. Reminding people our loved ones are all around us is wonderful. When they wake you up at 3:00 a.m., that may not be so wonderful.

There are several experiences that are not pleasant. Some loved ones that you encounter in Spirit form may not know they are deceased. Some may appear gruesome. Some may like to scare you because it is funny. Some may not know what is going on and are confused and take it out on you.

This one is hard to learn. You are in your Mind Body Reaction Faction. Your environment is off. You can't seem to understand why. You go through your Seven Spirit Communication Keys and you don't get a response. You have an urge to do something but there is nothing going on. It feels like the calm before the storm. What do you do when this happens? Pray and send love to the world. Over time, you will understand your reason for this experience. Spirit can't wait to show you.

There will be times when your friends or loved ones think you know everything. They will ask you a question and will not like Spirit's answer and take it out on you. This is when to decide how you want to have a boundary with your friends. I had a friend, Anna, who begged and begged me for a reading. She wanted to connect so bad with her Auntie.

I gave in and granted the reading against my better judgement. I asked for guidance from Spirit and was told to proceed with the reading but the friendship was over. I fought Spirit for two weeks before I gave in.

Right before the reading, I was told that Anna needed to hear what I had to say. I was to be blunt and say exactly word for word what Spirit said. I agreed and kindly asked Spirit to literally spell it out for me.

How was it spelled out? In old English with 'thees' and 'thys.' I asked for my modern English.

I prefaced the message with don't be mad at the messenger. This message was full of heartache and I needed Anna to be open to hearing it. The message for Anna was if you stay with him for any amount of time, you will not have a happy or long life. The pain he causes you now will seem like a tiny scratch if you stay any longer. You deserve more in life and there is happiness, just not with him. Time to leave with grace.

I explained that Spirit was watching out for her and that it was time for her to move on. Anna told me I wanted her man and got up and left. She then told me I was crazy.

Unfortunately, our friendship was over in that moment. I honored what Spirit asked me to do. I found out a few months later, Spirit finally got Anna to listen and she broke up with him. I missed Anna but was happy she moved forward with her life.

PAY IT FORWARD WITH SPIRIT'S LOVE

Once your Seven Spirit Communication Keys are in use, it will be your pleasure to pay it forward with Spirit's love. Scanning your environment will be faster and paying it forward of Spirit's love will be more fun. After you scan a room, for example, you will understand where your energy may be directed or where the love needs to be filled in. This will help you to help Spirit.

My husband and I were flying back from Las Vegas. When we arrived at the airport, Spirit told me to speak with the flight attendant and let them know we would be willing to take a different flight if we both could be bumped to another flight. The flight attendant graciously smiled and said okay, sheepishly. She verified and the flight was not overbooked, so she didn't see that she would need to accommodate my request. I graciously requested we be first if this situation happens.

We boarded our flight and made some friends with those around us. We found out the people next to us were heading back to Australia but had to go to LAX. I told them I would love to visit there. They were hoping their friend could catch the flight with them or he would be bumped for the LAX to Australia flight. The flight was full.

I told them, we would bump our flight and let their friend have our seat if the flight attendant would give us a new flight for free. They could not believe we would do this for them. Total strangers. We were all excited.

One man explained the situation to the flight attendant. After about ten minutes of figuring out how to make this happen, the flight attendant came up to us and said, "I'm sorry but we need to bump you both to another flight. Your seat belt is not secure and we have a passenger that only needs one seat." We told her we were happy to bump our flight. All the Australians made it to the flight together.

We ended up spending another night in Las Vegas. The hotel, flight change, and dinner were free. If I didn't listen to Spirit, we would not have had another night in Vegas and made new friends from Australia. We needed both.

MEETING PLACE FOR HOUSING INFORMATION
– MIND PALACE CREATION

There is a lot of information to process. How will you remember all this information while working with Spirit? Creating a mind palace with Spirit is a fantastic way to house your information with Spirit. You mind palace is also a place for you to create space to meet with Spirit to connect. While in a meditative state, create an environment that you enjoy – a mind palace.

A mind palace only has the limits of your imagination. This is a safe space for you to create a location to house all your Spirit experiences. This will allow you to reference that information at any time. How do I remember what I house? Over time and repetitive actions of creating your mind palace, you will devise a unique mind palace. Start out by imagining that you are meeting Spirit and your guides in one location for meditation. This place is where you want to go to get questions answered from Spirit, as well as understanding your communication with Spirit on a deeper level. Trust me, you are ready. With all the Spirit interaction you have had in your life, this will make it easier.

The mind palace can be anything you want it to look like. Right now, create a space in your mind of your favorite room or location. Start using attributes from that room to start your mind palace. When I want Spirit to meet me there, I send a prayer request to do so. Sometimes I play a certain song and ask Spirit to join me. Explain to Spirit that when you listen to a specific song, the mind palace is open for us to have a deep discussion. This has been wonderful for me to connect with Spirt and my guides when I am confused or do not understand the message that I am receiving.

Spirit has infinite knowledge and I know I won't remember everything. When you meditate, give it time and trust in Spirit. Have fun with creating your mind palace. This is an additional way to understanding each guide's communication style. I have one guide that thinks everything is funny while another guide does not and is serious. Yes, it is serious work but it can also be fun. The foundation of your mind palace – and the best way to grow it – is to keep it simple, judgment-free, joyful, and with gratitude. Spirit communication stream will flowing and not stop. It's all for you to be your best. That is what Spirit wants for you.

4

THE ONE WITH KEYS TO SPIRIT FOUNDATION

"Religion is belief in someone else's experience. Spirituality is having your own experience."

— DEEPAK CHOPRA

I am walking right now through this experience with you. You no longer have to hold your breath and hope enough time passes so you may be filled with wisdom to know what to do next. There's no need for that. You picked up this text and read it for a reason.

Just as Deepak Chopra said, you are having an experience. I just happened to have had that experience prior to yours, and now I'm here to share with you what key steps to take to fill you up with a treasure chest of keys that unlock the gifts Spirit has blessed your life with.

SPIRIT'S SEVERAL NAMES

There are so many ways to travel. Every person is different. I'm different than you are and you are from me. This path I'm about to share with you is one of the first paths I took on my experience in service to Spirit. I have experienced first-hand how Spirit's love is your number one absolute fantastic, grace filled, music filled, humble filled, and powerful key. Spirit's Love Key is your everything. (If God is not the noun you prefer, simply use the word you are most comfortable with. I use Spirit because I feel it covers all my bases – Universal Love.) This is just a blueprint for the foundation of your mind palace that we are building that holds all the keys you will ever need or want. This is endless. Throughout this book I will be referring to God as Spirit.

Spirit's love is all around and it never stops. Even when we are confused in our circumstances, it will be one of our most important relationships to cultivate. I know you already have a connection and a belief system set in place. What we are doing right now is adding on to that – not changing it. In order for this communication connection to work, you need to believe not me, not your dog, or your cat – you. What feels good? How do you feel grounded? When you have that choice made, own it for that moment.

I interchange the nouns all the time. I like to keep my options open and make it fun. Sometimes, I call God, Sky Daddy. Make this fun. If you make this fun, trust me, connecting will be so much easier and more playful. Laughter instantly raises your vibration, and makes your mood elevated and joyful.

SPIRIT IS LOVE. LOVE IS SPIRIT

The relationship love you have and belief you have is the main key. This is the Spirit's Love Key that you will call on for everything. No action should be taken by you unless this love is connected first. There are many reasons for this and the two main reasons I'll touch on.

Spirit's Love Key, one, is the energy state you can help yourself and others best in. Two, safety: if you are going to make a steak, you don't go buy chicken. You buy a steak. You have to set yourself up to prepare for steak making. This is the same for getting your mind/ body/ spirit in order for connection. How do you do that? I don't have hours to meditate and connect to Spirit. I have a busy life, I have kids, a significant other, work, and friends to take care of – how could you ask me to take time for Spirit's Love Key? The more you build your relationship with Spirit, the more connections will flow at the pace you need, when you need. This does take time and practice. Spirit is ready when you are.

PACE

Yes, in the beginning I need you to take the pace slow. I mean S, to the L, to the O, to the W. And breathe. Imagine a sloth, slowly crossing the street. I need you to take it slow so you have the energy – slow so you understand the different ways Spirit is talking to you. If we do this fast or quick, then the messages are more difficult to decipher. Remember that old game that you played when you were in grade school, Operator? If the girl spoke too fast because she was excited to share the message, the message got all jumbled and we had no idea what the original message was. It is the same with Spirit.

Spirit travels at speeds we cannot interpret with our human minds. In our connect to Spirit, we are lifting ourselves to their speed or vibration. If we slow our energy, heartbeat, and breathing, we can elevate our minds to connecting to their energy. They are just as excited to speak to us, so when we tell them – via meditating or quiet mind sitting – we are telling Spirit, "I'm connecting with you with slow, calming energy." We also start our prayers of connection with them. Also, in the beginning, think about how you want to connect with Spirit. Do you want to hear, see, feel? For myself, in the beginning, I did not want to hear things outside of my head. It was too much for me to process.

VISUAL REQUEST

One time, I thought I was being cool and said, "Hey Spirit, I'm ready to see you. Yup, I'm ready." Nothing happened. I have no idea why I thought it would be instant. "Spirit! Yes, I can take it. I'm ready to see you." I was confident. One night, I woke up and had to use the bathroom. I walked in the bathroom and turned on the light, and the next thing I knew, I was diving for the floor because I thought there was a stranger in my bathroom.

When I went to turn on the light, my Grandpa Bill was standing in the mirror, as if he was peeking through a window on a warm summer day. All he did was wave a hand hi and smile. I was not ready. Well, I was, but I thought Spirit was going to have like a coming out party – like a huge presentation. No, in the middle of the night, you will see Spirit. It took me a few days to process that experience. I did have several questions. They were answered but it took several years for the answers because I didn't know what to do.

I don't want you diving on the floor in the middle of the night and pissing off the downstairs neighbor or waking up the dog just because you asked to talk to Spirit and you got scared. I laugh about it now, but it was not the best way to talk to Spirit. You see, the energy I gave out is the energy I got back. It was from ego – not from the heart, not from love. The Law of Attraction is real. What you put out, you are already receiving back.

The energy I gave to Spirit is the energy I'm going to get back. When you are centered or grounded, you are setting your body, mind, and spirit up for connection. There are keys and how you learn them first is slow and at your centered energy level. Breathing is the first step in Spirit's Love Key because Spirit gave you the breath of life. When you bow your head and feel the nape of your neck, that is the place that Spirit placed his breath upon you. Go ahead and feel the nape of your neck again. When you need to connect and center, take a breath and bow your head.

BREATHING TO CONNECT TO YOUR SPIRIT COMMUNICATION

Breathe in for four seconds.

Hold and feel the breath for seven seconds. Where does your body need to relax?

Exhale for eight seconds.

Feel breath. Is your body relaxed?

This step will take some mastering. I know it's just breathing. When someone is speaking to you, it sometimes takes time to adjust your energy to theirs. Breath is the way to connect. There is no quieting the mind. We are connecting the mind. Like looking through a kaleidoscope, the images are blurry at first, and you need to take a few moments to understand what you are interpreting. Then you move to the light and have a better grasp of what beautiful, sacred geometry you are looking at. This is the same.

When you breathe, it seems like it has a beautiful

rhythm and it feels amazing. That is the feeling of being in Spirit's love. You have set your path to connecting with Spirit and all Spirit's love. The Spirit's Love Key governs the rest of the keys that will be created for your mind palace.

MIND PALACE

Cultivating your mind palace is a great technique I've used to communicate with Spirit. To create a mind palace, it starts with imagination. Take some time to think about a place that gives you everything you need all at once, from the outside landscaping to the inside chair that you sit on. It can be anything you want. For myself, I have a cozy room by a fireplace with two chairs. I picture speaking with Spirit there when I meditate. There is also space for a filing system for communicating with Spirit.

The mind palace can be anything you want, at any time, and it is also a way to elevate your mind to communicate to Spirit. The mind palace is a working tool for you to use.

When we activate the Spirit's Love Key, this is our call to Spirit that we are ready to communicate. Now, before we ask for communication, we need to set an intention for this connection. I mean you don't just call up your friend Jimmy and not talk to him. You had a reason or an intention to call Jimmy. This is the same with Spirit. This is the Intention Key.

THE INTENTION KEY

The Intention Key is the second most important key in our mind palace as it is foundational. What information do you need to help yourself, so you may help others? How can I be of service to myself, my child, husband, wife, sister, brother, friend, colleague, or client who has come to me for guidance? State, "I am here, Spirit. Please put your message in my energy so I may be of service." The main ingredient for the Intention Key is love. If love is not the reason, then we need to go back to breathing until love is the main ingredient. Without love, the correct message from Spirit will not be received.

A baseball player going up to bat does not hit a home run every time. He has to take a few swings, feel the dirt. Feel the bat. Sometimes he needs a time out and asks the ref for one. He settles himself for the best stance. This is the same for Spirit. The main action is setting up for success. The foundation work is the hardest to establish, and you feel like you are all over the place. From now on, we will be setting up the architecture for your mind palace to house the Keys. After we have it all set up, you can add on, or redecorate. It is up to you and it will be great.

For the mind palace architecture, the Keys are Spirit's Love and The Intention. The combination of you and Spirit's Love with Intention is your sacred, one of a kind vibration. When you have an elevated vibration, you feel happy and light. When your vibration is low, you feel heavy and slow. Understand that your high vibration is full of love and service: Spirit's grace at its finest.

You are responsible for yourself. You are also responsible for your own energy. If I took the following actions: walked into your room, slammed the door, huffed, sat down, and didn't say a word – what would you think is going on? What would you ask me? You would say something like that I was upset by the way I walked in door.

I created that energy before I walked through your door. You are responsible for your energy. You are responsible for your energy at all times. This is the same when Spirit connects. If we connect with healthy Spirit love intention, that karma is already coming back to us. Our thoughts do become things after we think them. You thought I was mad when I walked in the door. Spirit feels the same. When we have built and cultivated ourselves to do our best with our set intensions, we grow.

Everything in our world and planet is giving off a vibration. That new music you just bought – it brought you joy when you purchased it. Our loving something puts our energy on it. Our energy vibration is all around us. It varies in size but averages ten feet completely around us. Like a ball, we are in the middle of our vibration at all times. You image hearing that music live and when the music artist hits the stage, they fill that stage with their vibrations, energy, love. The artists want you to feel their response to you.

Our vibrations get dirty, just like our bodies, so we need to clean them up. Using the two foundation architecture keys – Spirit's Love Key and the Intention Key – is a way to do so. (Hey, by the way, I'm glad we are here doing this together. It's so much better than doing this on your own.) At any time during use, any of your keys may revert back to Key Reset.

If you don't get any information from the questions, you ask the following.

How can I help?

What is best for this situation or person?

The Key Reset is to shake off whatever is your obstacle right now. Shake off the energy right now. If you can't shake it, I want you to put it in your hand right now and walk over to the garbage and throw it away. You don't want to go to the garbage. Go open the front door and hand it over to the Holy Spirit because Spirit sent him to take that blockage from you. The Key Reset returns you to breath and to the intention.

KEY RESET

If you are having issues connecting, here are a few tips to get your mind/ body connection adjusted. You may sing a song or listen to your favorite song. Music is a key as it can lift up and tweak our minds out of the gutter and place us back on the road. Another way for an instant pick-me-up is laughter. Comedian Milton Berle said, "The quickest way to a vacation is laughter." I have used laughter in several ways to lighten the mood.

Once I was at the Los Angeles (LAX) airport. I was in line for an international flight and there were ten rows of zig zag line to get through security. The attendant took all the ropes that keep the ten rows in order and dropped them all. There were no more lines. We were all one mass of people.

After she had everyone back up out of the way because they needed to add more rope for more people. The entire line of people didn't want to move because they didn't want to lose their place in line. The tension in the air was angry and I was not happy either. I did what I did best.

I dropped my head asked Spirit to fill the room with love and kindness compassion. I asked that we all make our flights and we all get back in line and all is good. The next thing I do – which is something I never do – I started singing Gwen Stefani's song "Crash" – the lyric "Back it up." I sang it like it was from the gospel and Ms. Whitney Houston was taking me there with Gwen's song. You see no one in the line was moving. The airline attendants couldn't make anyone move. Once I started singing it over and over the crowd – yes, a large crowd – 75 percent of the crowd joined and we sang together the lyric. We all clapped for each other and laughed. It instantly changed the room. We all complimented each other. We bonded.

Bonded through music and love. Thanks Spirit, Gwen, and Whitney.

This will take practice. You will add to it as you adjust and grow your connection to Spirit. We have the base of your foundation set. There are several ways of communication. You know now that meditation and intention are how you set yourself up. Now Spirit has never-ending energy, so they have several different way they communicate to each other and to us. It's been broken down to general ways. Each person is different, so be curious to understand how Spirit knew you would pick up on your end.

MEDIUM DEFINED

A medium is a person who sits on the bridge of life that is in between the physical planet (Earth) and the ethereal Spirit world. A medium opens both ends of the bridge to congregate the messages from the ethereal spirit world to our physical plane earth. A medium is a person who reads the energy vibration of those whose physical body dies and whose soul transitions out of the body.

A medium focuses on the vibration of a soul's time here on earth. They can sense the vibrational energy of loved ones from the other side. Through meditation, a medium raises their vibration to connect to the vibration of Spirit. Once connected to Spirit, then the loved ones from the earthly plane start to communicate. All mediums are psychic. Psychics are specifically given a special intuitive gift to read the energy imprints from people, places, and things. They have the ability to read the energy from the past, present, and future. Psychics grow their intuitive energy gifts by intentions and practice. Psychics are not able to raise their vibration to connect with Spirit's vibration so they are not able to connect with our loved ones that have passed. This is why not all psychics are mediums.

Psychics and mediums are governed by the same laws of the universe. Spirit knew you had the beautiful unique love, intelligence, and strength to receive messages. I'm not into labels but for myself, I am a psychic medium. You are a psychic medium.

Now, you have your two key mind palace foundations set and you understand that you are a psychic medium.

What are the different ways Spirit communicates to you?

Clear Knowing – A strong sense or thought that a specific experience or answer is given to you by Spirit and you have no doubt.

Senses – Spirit will use your sight, sound, smell, taste, and feel sense to communicate to you. Visual – Spirit will give you a short movie gif, or snapshot pictures to give you faster communication for you to understand the messages.

Colors – Spirit will use colors to get your attention for communication.

Numbers – Spirit will use numbers to communicate to let you know you are on the best path.

Your Life Stories – Spirit will use your life experiences to give you a message. It gets your attention and is a shortcut to message giving.

Later on, I'll take you through what this all means but for now, how does Spirit communicate to you? You see, our brains are like computers, and we have to program them to link with Spirit – and our senses are how to interpret that communication.

5

THE ONE WITH SPIRIT
AWAKENING YOUR
MEDIUM TYPE

"There is no fear in love; instead, love drives out fear, because fear involves punishment. So the one who fears is not complete in love."

— 1 JOHN 4:18

We have established that you are a psychic medium but for the remainder of the book, I'll refer to you as a medium. It's just easier for understanding your mediumship gifts from Spirit. Now Spirit assessed you and your personality and how you learn. He also sent you helpers. Think of these helpers as guardians of the message and also communication assistance energies. I like to call them Spirit guides. These Spirit guides help you understand who you are on the earth plane. So it's best to guide the communication through Spirit's love to your heart to take action or to pray.

GUIDES

Through the Natural Law – like attracts like – your Spirit guides are attracted to not only your energy but your moral and ethical code. They also see how you may both grow together to serve humankind with love. Your Spirit Guides assist you in every sense and in every way. They are nudged from Spirit to understand what the best way for you is to receive information.

We all have our own reality and we all have our own way of interpreting our environment. There are two ways you may have communicated – or both, in some cases. First of all, Spirit is trying to get your attention. You know, like when the puppy at the park runs right up to you because you brought a new energy and they want to see what you are all about. This is the same with loved ones that would like to speak to us through Spirit and His love.

The first way to get your attention is in the material world – something physically will happen on the earth plane to grab your attention and force you to bear witness to a miracle – by manifesting a movement of energy that you can witness. I know you have a list of times or "ghost stories" of times of the past where someone, somewhere, saw something that cannot be explained. This list of stories gives us a clue to how you interpret data from Spirit and what your experiences are like. We are going to put on our detective persona on and do some research on you and your experiences.

Before we do that, let's talk about the two types of mediums. There are mental mediums and there are phys-ical mediums. The mental medium is able to interpret messages from the Spirit world to the earthly plane. The physical mediums have the physical ability in their biology to create ectoplasm with connection of Spirit and His love.

For the purposes of this book, we will mainly focus on mental mediums – as those are most of your experiences as they have brought you here.

MENTAL MEDIUM DEFINED

The mental medium is using what we spoke of in Chapter 4 – the two main keys of the foundation of your mind palace: Spirit's Love and Intention Key. The combinations of these keys will grow just like a muscle that is strengthening over time. It will be from Spirit and you will have exercises to do so your communication strengthens over time.

The mental and physical mediums use daily mediation, weekly group mediation (not necessary in the beginning stages if you can't find one), affirmations, tarot cards, wands, pendulums, music, Spiritual coaching, channeling, and astrology to name a few.

One example is exercise and healthy eating. Oh yes, hydration is key to this because energy will have a hard time moving if you don't have water keeping you going. When working with Spirit on a daily basis, an adjustment needs to happen with your water and food intake. You are reading and moving energy and it takes fuel – water and food.

These rituals are extremely important because they fuel your relationship with Spirit. They need to know what is going on in your life to connect in the time and space you need them to. Just like in the last chapter, I was diving on the ground because I wanted to see spirit material in front of me. That request was a form of physical mediumship. My intention was strong and Spirit got my attention. Now I almost had a heart attack in the moment for a few reasons. One, I did not have a good connection with Spirit because I was from a place of fear not love. My energy was like, "Come on, show me who you are, Spirit." Immediately, Grandpa Bill was in the mirror. Two, I did not ask how, where, when to send me the answer. What I had was a nasty request and it was answered in a nasty way.

When you establish rituals with Spirit, they know your energy. They know you need them and are waiting to assist you so you may assist yourself. This bond grows. What type of medium are you? The majority of mediums start out as a mental medium and realize down their journey they are also physical mediums too. Trust me, you want to take this slow and find out who you are as a medium. Slowly learn what your energy can do to help and assist you to help others in need.

After you construct and set a daily time to connect with Spirit, what do you do? Refer back to Chapter 4.

JOURNEY

On my journey, I had no idea what was going on and who was talking to me. I noticed the same thing came into my reality over and over again. I was living proof of *Groundhog Day*. If you are not understanding what Spirit is saying, they will keep repeating it to you. The universe keeps sending you the message in different ways and you will see what it is all aboutrepetition.

If you find yourself frustrated and going nowhere, ask Spirit for signs that you are on the right path of communication. Then relax and watch the miracles unfold before your eyes. What you just did right now is reset yourself full of love and not fear. This is part of the journey with Spirit.

MY HOLY GHOST

In addition to repetition, what are your experiences? For myself, I didn't realize I was speaking to Spirit until I was eleven years old. Let me back up a bit. My first memory is playing in my crib with my buddy. I would stand up and he would stand outside the crib. He would wave to me and tell me things. Then I would see him float through a wall. The love I felt in that memory was powerful. It felt like home, a fuzzy feeling when you can rest from a long day of working or school. I was always so happy to see him. I saw him in more than one place and with several different people. I would have discussions, great chats, and giggle. I remember his singing was not particularly good and I thought it was funny.

Fast forward to eleven years old when I was at a family gathering. I went to sit down next to my friend, my buddy. I never had a name for him. He was my buddy. That is what I called him and I found it so sweet that Buddy was the first word I ever spoke.

I had just fixed my plate of food and saw my buddy and he waved to me. I nodded back that would signal to him I would head on over to him and eat next to him. I did just that. I was all seated in my chair at the table and not much was said. Just your normal exchange when people are eating, chit and chatting all around. I leaned over to ask my buddy a question when my cousin sat right on top of my buddy. I never blinked so much in my life. I thought I was in a dream.

What the hell just happened? I was eating a bite of food and immediately my buddy is there and now he's not. Where the hell did my cousin come from? The energy I saw was like a sparkle cloud emanating light that got dispersed back into the ethereal plane. My cousin had no reaction to my buddy at all – as if he was not there at all. My buddy was sat on and disappeared. Whaaaaaat?

That was the moment I remember the story of Jesus' ascension to heaven. One minute his physical body was there and three days later he was gone. I felt in that moment, Spirit was showing me he was alive, just in a different form – the form of my buddy. Then it occurred to me my mind was pulling up all the times I was with my buddy in groups. We never spoke. If we were going to, he would walk away. No, not walk away, – glide away. Then my aha moment came – I did expect a group of angels to sing, but that was not the case. My buddy is a ghost spirit. I stopped eating.

I got scared and confused, and that moment was the last time I would directly interact with my buddy without fear for five years. In those five years, I had so many more experiences to share.

Oh yeah, my buddy I found out was my Grandpa Bill. Grandpa Bill died a year before I was born. I never saw a picture of him up close. The only picture displayed of Grandpa Bill showed him wearing this garment that looked like he was a knight from the round table. The picture was a full body picture so his face was small and it was taken back in the day. Also, the same picture was displayed in many houses but no one ever said who that was. I just thought he was some guy people liked in that outfit with a feather hat and sword with a black cape.

One day, I was organizing pictures with my Gram – Grandpa Bill's wife. There was a picture of a man in a boat with a little kid's sun hat on. I asked my Gram who that was. She said, "That is Bill." I said, "Who is Bill?" "Your Grandpa." I said, "Where is he?" Then she told me the story of how he passed. I held her hand and we said a prayer for him. Gram told me that is who we visit at the gravesite. I said, "What?" I remembered that several times in the year, we would go to the cemetery. We picked flowers from her garden to bring to him. I cut extras for other graves but that's for another time.

I could tell my Gram missed him. I could feel the bond of love between them both. It was beautiful and I hoped someone would love me unconditionally like that.

The next picture Gram showed me I literally fell off the footstool I was sitting on. The next picture was my buddy. My spirit buddy. I said, "Grandpa Bill is the boogey man that I always see in your house." I never told her that I would play with him all the time or how I ate waffles with him. I thought that was just for me and him. I got over my fear pretty quickly because of my Grandpa Bill's love.

My Gram never asked me about him. She never doubted that I played with him. I asked her why she didn't tell me stories about him. My Gram said that she would and did but I would correct her during the story telling with facts that Grandpa Bill liked. I remember saying to myself, "No one touches my soul like Spirit."

Take some time to journal about your experiences. Reviewing them later is a joy.

ALL SENSES INTERPRETATION

Your lizard brain interprets sensory communications by scanning your environment for cohesiveness. If there is imbalance in our environment, our minds direct our bodies to that imbalance for resolution. Our senses give us information all the time about the environment we are in. Our senses and our energy together are constantly scanning for if we choose fight or flight. Our senses also give us automatic reminders of the past which can be of equal use for Spirit to communicate to you.

IN MEDIUMSHIP THERE ARE SYMBOLS

When I smell lilacs, I instantly think of my Gram. Smelling lilacs can be used as a symbol between Spirit and myself for many different reasons. Those reasons would be for you both to decide. For example, lilacs as a symbol could represent grandmother energy, or lilacs could make you happy. If Spirit communicates lilacs to me, it symbolizes grandmother energy.

Scan your senses and learn to know your senses well. Know when something is off with your senses that is not your normal everyday feeling or focus. When I was in college, I thought for sure I had a Spirit around me that kept itching my forearm. I processed through my Seven Spirit Communication Keys and I was not able to get a connection from Spirit. I was so confused. The next day I was getting my medical physical and the doctor asked me about the eczema on my forearm. He explained that there was lotion to help with the extreme dry skin. Here I thought I'm so cool, I have a Spirit hanging around me for a few days. Nope, I had dry skin – I laughed. I know now to check senses regularly and when I don't, I end up laughing at myself.

What senses are being used to communicate to you from Spirit? When Spirit communicates using your senses, it's like giving you a fast, symbolic message almost like a shortcut. It is sometimes easier to get our attention with our senses. For example, my eyes were used when seeing my Grandpa Bill. I can see Spirit – visual. I would hear Spirit – auditory. I would feel the love of Spirit – feeling. I did not taste anything but tasting. The last but not least is a clear knowing. I call that the automatic message from Spirit – you just know. No questions asked or even thought of. Clear knowing is comparable to knowing that you love a person, pet, place, or thing. You know for a fact in your time and place. "I know."

Your senses and working with Spirit will evolve over time as you do. It's a great way to have fun and open to symbols with Spirit.

ASKS

There are so many different ways to receive a message from Spirit. I'm asked a lot, "How do you know that information? When did you find out?" This is why your mind palace is so useful. You will be able to catalog virtually with your mind all the different life experiences for Spirit to reference so you may receive the clearest message. Remember, like our fingerprints there are different ways to communicate and understand the message. I also use logic and realize: Spirit just placed that in my head for me to say to you and it comes from a place of love.

KNOWING

For example, I was driving with my husband and we came upon a sixteen-car accident. It looked like one car stopped short and the next fifteen cars hit one after the other. As we drove by, the first car looked like an accordion, the way it was smooshed. I took a breath and yelled at my husband to stop the car because it was my aunt's car. He said, "You don't know that. We haven't seen her new car." I said, "Well, it's not new anymore because that car is totaled." I asked him to pull over so I would be able to ask the police. He was not comfortable stopping to interrupt the police and fire fighters cleaning up what remained of the cars. I wasn't happy but understood if every person did that it would delay help. I prayed for those in that accident.

I prayed for that person in the car who I thought was my aunt. I prayed for all those people affected by the car accident. I prayed for us to drive safely. I prayed for my aunt that she was ok if that was her car and I would call her later in the day.

Three days later I received a call that my aunt indeed caused the car accident. She was saved by a miracle and made a full recovery of some bumps and bruises. After I shared the news with my husband, he never questioned me again.

This will take time and Spirit exercise. This is why maintaining your relationship with Spirit daily is so important. Trust me, this seems like a lot of what is going on. We are labeling your experiences and understandings how you best interpret Spirit., Congratulations, the Spirit communication is flowing steady. You know the different ways Spirit speaks through you as an instrument.

6

THE ONE WITH SPIRIT SPEAKING THROUGH YOUR SENSES

"The more knowledge, the more responsibility. The more love, the more ability."

— EDGAR CAYCE

What do your senses tell you about your key gifts from Spirit? First of all, the question is why is this happening to you? Why doesn't everyone have this gift? Long story short: Spirit placed a call and you answered. As all parts of life unfold, so do our gifts. This chapter we are going to get more in depth of Logic Key, Dream Key, Life Stories Key, chakras, and colors.

LOGIC KEY

You have had several medium experiences in your life. I want you to take yourself to the one experience you keep returning to – the one that keeps repeating because there is something there for you to learn. That is the one that will play a role in the Logic Key – what are my current gifts that I'm using and how are they used for communications?

Spirit will use a perfect tool – you. You have several body parts that can help with receiving communication with spirit. The mind is the first tool to connect with Spirit. Our minds are like computers; we are currently putting new data in your reality and processing it to fit your senses and your experiences. Later, we will see what matches with you at the present.

You are prepped for scanning your environment for things that don't match up. Or if there is an unbalance of energy in the room. Or if there is some area that you want to stay away from. You are constantly doing this to keep your body safe. We all do this. We all have an energy and we decide if we want to exercise it or not. Different people are different. We all learn differently and we all receive communication differently. For example, we all have different finger prints – no two are the same – that is the same with Spirit. They communicate to us in the beginning in way that is easy first.

The Logic Key is a check and balance of your communication and environment with Spirit and for speaking to your loved ones on the earth. When experiencing Spirit Communication, the Logic Key is a must. The Logic Key is used to determine a deeper meaning of your Spirit Communication and deciphering the message. For example, a feather floats on my path just as I was thinking about my friend Adam who loves birds. I want to use the Logic Key to determine if I'm getting a message from Spirit or not.

Here are a series of questions to assist you with the Logic Key:

- Travel back in your mind. What is the last thing I was thinking before I saw the feather?
- What was the thought before that?
- Is there a link between number one and number two?
- Is there an explanation for the feather on your path?
- If you find a link in your thinking, then your mind is simply thinking about your friend and the feather reminded you of them.
- If there is no link, then it is time to ask Spirit for further information.

The Logic Key is using common sense in observing your mind, thoughts, and links between experiences. For example, there was a cold chill in the air while I was sitting on the couch the other day. I looked around in my environment and saw that the window was not closed properly and thus the cold chill. As we grow our knowledge base in science, art, music, philosophy, etcetera, our Logic Key grows. In the beginning, we will logic away messages from Spirit because we simply cannot believe it could be that simple. The Logic Key is ever evolving, as you do, with Spirit.

LOGICAL RADIO SIGNAL

In college, I had an apartment and my husband (boyfriend at the time) would visit me on the weekends. Sean had an electric guitar with an amplifier. Thursday, the day before he arrived, the amplifier started talking to me. I heard a man's voice. It was not clear. I thought, "This is new."

Spirit knows I don't like hearing Spirits out loud. I started asking questions but was not able to find out what was going on. I thought for sure this is Spirit communication. I am 100 percent sure. The amplifier was not turned on at all. How could this be happening? Then, when I said, "I give up," it stopped. "Tomorrow, I'm going to ask Sean about it."

The next day, we were back at the apartment and I had just explained what my amplifier experience. I told him maybe we can try again to see if the Spirit will come through. Sean and I checked out the guitar and the amplifier and realized how this was happening.

I was living right across the street from the local radio and news station. We quickly figured out that the amplifier was picking up a radio signal and playing partial waves that sounded like speaking. We moved the amplifier around the room and closer to the station, the better the voice sounded. We had figured out that it wasn't Spirit at all – it was a radio signal.

TWO LOGIC VERIFICATIONS

Spirit never responded to communicate. I went through my senses and nothing from Spirit.

We moved the amplifier and the same speaking played and realized it was the radio station.

It would have been easy to keep pushing the Spirit connection, but it felt off. There also may be times when you feel that a Spirit is literally touching your leg or arm in a light way. It takes a lot of Spirit's energy to make you feel their presence on your skin. Having been a medium for over four decades, Spirit would want your attention in a big way to touch you. In most cases, people assume a ghost is touching them without permission but our vagus nerve, when stimulated, will tell your mind that someone is touching you, when in fact the vagus nerve is overly stimulated. The vagus nerve runs through our whole body. If you are an active person, this is more likely to be why you have the feeling someone is touching your leg.

SPIRIT BOUNDARY

When I got serious about growing my relationship with Spirit, it filled me up. I found I loved to be of service. I had to share what my boundaries are with Spirit. I told Spirit, "Please don't send Spirits in physical form. I will die of a heart attack and then I'll be on your side. I wouldn't be able to help anyone."

It stopped immediately and I felt a warm breeze sweep over me. I was standing inside my home and there was no breeze or fan on. Then I remembered Spirit's love growing. I knew He loved me before and now I feel His love. I felt so humbled. When you state your boundary, know that Spirit hears you. I needed a sign because I wasn't sure what I was doing in the beginning. After cultivating your relationship, you will know when Spirit is present.

When I give details of my boundary to Spirit, I think of explaining my boundary to a toddler. I am simple in my language and clear about what I will not accept. For example, I was driving home from college and it was a four-hour drive. It was at night and dark. The radio was playing and I was humming along. A light out of the corner of my left eye had me turn my head. When I turned my head, Spirit decided to appear in the window and say hi. I screamed so loud, Sean jumped up from a sleep and thought we hit a car because I swerved. I regained control of my swerve and yelled at the Spirit for scaring me.

It was time to stop for gas and a perfect time to collect myself. I sat in the car and had a pray chat. I explained that was to never happen again to me or any other person. It was not funny. The Spirit was doing their best because their loved one was working at the gas station and they wanted to give a message. I told them I wasn't going to go in there and give a message like that. I kindly asked what they wanted to tell their loved one and it was that they loved them.

I went inside to pay for the gas and there was only one person working and I knew the message was for her. I asked Spirit to guide me as I paid for the gas. I saw she had a tattoo on her forearm and I complimented the art and tattoo style. I asked, "What was her inspiration for the tattoo?" She said it was in honor of her father. I looked her in the eye and said, "Wow, what a beautiful tattoo to honor someone who loved you so much. What a beautiful reminder of love." She looked at me and teared up and said, "Yes, he did love me. I never thought of him loving me as a symbol as well for my tattoo." She thanked me and asked if she could give me a hug.

Normally, at eleven at night I don't like to stop for gas and chat about tattoos but that was my experience. I was grateful to give Spirit's message and glad I was open after being scared. To this day, Spirits do not scare me while I'm driving.

DREAM KEY

According to The Society of Analytical Psychology of Carl Jung, "Jung saw dreams as the psyche's attempt to communicate important things to the individual, and he valued them highly, perhaps above all else, as a way of knowing what was going on."

I had to think, "How would I want grandpa Bill to talk to me about extreme life events?" I immediately thought dreams – and Dream Key was created. I asked Spirit to give me clear messages in my dreams. I wanted to understand myself to help others. I have studied dreams since I was able to journal about my dreams; we are talking decades. It took a lot of brain training and sleep but man, dream messages are fun, cool, exciting, and confusing. That is why you need to know what your dream definitions are. What and who is your energy while in a dream state?

That is your first assignment. Who are you in your dreams? Are you passive in your dreams? Do you watch your dreams like a movie? Do you participate in your dreams? Do your loved ones visit you in your dreams? If so ,what do they say to you? What do your loved ones do in the dreams?

If you just said like me, "I don't remember my dreams," then stop. You are thinking too literally for me right now. Hold up. Let's define what dream is. A dream is, in medical terms, your brainwaves in a certain pattern and your eyes moving rapidly and we deduce you are sleeping and your mind is resting so you can gather energy for the morning. Yes, that is one part of the Dream Key I refer to.

The second dream definition is while you are awake and conscious your mind wanders over to a new thought experience. You take your time and say, "Yeah, I have to run that errand later but first I need to go to the bank and get cash because I need that for tomorrow and it would be on the way. If I do that, then I should go grab a new yoga mat because there is a sale at the boutique." Then you take a breath and decide – "Do I want to do all that?" You come back in your body and realize you are at the stoplight in California and have listened through an entire song on the radio and the green arrow is lit and you are not moving. That is what some people refer to as "daydreams." I call them dreams – a different state of consciousness.

When we choose to allow our minds to go in that flow of altered state, we have to have good communication with our dreams and daydreams. The dreams you have with Spirit interaction and non-Spirit interaction are all important because they are about you and your life's journey. When you are using your dreams to communicate with Spirit, that energy flow, dream definitions, symbols, and meanings will grow into knowings: specific messages about specific experiences, past, present, or future visions.

We are growing our communication with Spirit. There is so much data coming at us – how do we understand? It's time for questions. You have this dream or daydream. Is this dream repetitive? How often do I dream this? Is there a particular time of year? Life event? Do I need to do something? What does Spirit want me to do? How can I be of help with this information? If you are not sure about these answers, you can do muscle testing. Let it go and come back and see if you get a different answer. Move to a different part of the room to get it organized.

Scan your mind right now? What image is represented over and over in my dreams? Sometimes over time, people, animals, places, and things repeat. The Logic Key is so important and so is growing that dream muscle. The main question – when using Logic Key and the Dream Key – is what is going on in your life right now that pertains to this current dream? If what is going on in your life is in the dream, then you know your mind is processing. If the other part of the dream doesn't have any part of your life, there may be a message from Spirit.

I will take you through my Dream Key journey and how I used the Logic Key along the path. I have studied dreams my whole life and have read several books for the interpretation of them. With the experiences I've had with dreams, I would have to write a whole other book series for that. For now, we will focus on the foundation for your Logic Key.

Yes, is it good to read about dreams, of course. Growing is encouraged. However, I want you to have in the front of your mind when reading any text that you may not agree or resonate with all the information but there will be nuggets of wisdom that pull your focus. Hold onto those. Also, the information you receive from reading the book about dreams and symbols is that author's definition of what that symbol means to them.

Yes, there are overlapping symbols that a lot of psychics and mediums use. That is because they taught each other the same symbols to use with Spirit. That resonated over decades of sharing this knowledge. One of the top symbols I have been taught, like so many before, "red balloons" means a celebration is coming for the person. If you hate the color red or balloons, you have free will to change those meanings for you and your Spirit communication. When you celebrate someone, what is your symbol for that? Play with Spirit development.

For myself, I don't have red balloons as my celebration symbol; I have a confetti symbol. In the beginning, it was red balloons because that is what I read. As I worked with Spirit, it evolved. This will happen for you. When we get to that point, it is so much fun to use your imagination with Spirit. We need to establish the basic terms first.

Spirit uses colors to help communicate. Again, you can go through colors: red, orange, yellow, green, blue, indigo, purple – which are also your chakra colors. Chakras are energy points in areas of the body. Chakras have several layers of information for us to use to interpret Spirit. Chakras have musical notes colors to help us connect. This will help us when we exercise feeling Spirit and when on our bodies, we feel spirit.

This is the universal blueprint of chakras. Keeping yourself grounded with your charkas is a wonderful way to keep you moving. Yoga teachers speak about chakras and breathing during sessions. After working with Spirit deeper, you will add to your understanding of chakras to receive messages and to give messages. Using your Chakras will help when using your Logic Key.

LOGICAL TRACE

In addition, for understanding your environment, The Logic Key is here to help you trace the energy. This new symbol has appeared in my reality. What do I do with it? Put it on a holding shelf. You don't have enough data to interpret it. Keep journaling about it and you will soon see what the symbols meanings are to you.

For example, I would dream about running. Running all the time. My daydreams would be about running. This one summer, all I thought about was running. I was running up hill, downhill, it was crazy. For three months, all I wrote about was running. I finally saw the patterns which led me to what Spirit was communicating. At the end of that summer, our whole neighborhood changed. Neighbors moved; new people moved in. The people in our entire block were running. Our whole street seemed like busy ants making a new nest.

For my beginning, with the other journaling, I wrote down, "This is what the running symbol means to me. Running – moving, take action, going toward something, or going away from something." After years of working with Spirit, my symbol for running has evolved to this after a myriad of questions are answered.

RUNNING – QUESTIONING THE DREAM

What is your first response to the runner?

Am I running?

Who is running?

How many people are running?

Running scared or casual?

Am I just watching this like a movie on the screen?

Is the stop motion running just like watching a picture?

What colors are the runners wearing?

Is it clear or foggy?

What is the ground they are running on?

Is steady or rocky?

Wet or dry?

Is there a particular time of year you see with the runners?

What do you wish for the runner in this vision?

What assistance would they be able to use to move forward?

What is the best thing for the runner to know?

How do you want this runner to respond to your assistance?

What do they need from you to get to the goal they are running to?

Is the runner running backward?

Do you see the word run?

Do you see the word running backward?

When is the person running?

What are they wearing?

Is it from this time period or a different one?

Do you see the runner move toward or away?

Now there are several more questions I may add to understand the definition of running in my dreams but those are for me and wouldn't help you – as the questions are for me in depth and related to my experiences with Spirit.

The main questions to start with dream understanding is who, what, when, where. Who is in my dream? What is in my dream? When is my dream happening? Where is my dream? Do I go over all these questions when I get the symbol for running? The answer is yes and I add more as time goes on.

Why? Every encounter you have is like your fingerprint. You know you are reading words. You mind has been trained that this is a word. You will have a general definition with Spirit for running but each individual you have will have more details about running you need to get. When you allow your mind to wander around and ask every question you can think of, Spirit will answer you faster, stronger, and more accurately – but the bond has to be there to strengthen it.

This is one example of how you are going to establish your mind palace. All these keys make up your communication and your growth to establish your style of communication. After decades of cultivating my language with Spirit, it grows.

LIFE STORIES KEY

When you and Spirit have established a foundation for communication, finding that wonderful spot in your mind palace to congregate with Spirit is gratifying after all the hard work you have done. Over time – and with the practice of meditating with Spirit continually – Spirit will use your life stories or experiences to relay messages to you. This is the Life Stories Key.

Every area of your life contains a lot of information for Spirit to reference when communicating. This is the perfect opportunity to use a story that you are familiar with to understand the message from spirit. The Life Stories Key smacked me upside the head and got my attention.

While in college, a professor was pregnant with twins. Unfortunately, one of the twins' brains did not fully form. They found that she would not live long after the birth. I prayed for the entire family. It was a beautiful celebration of life. Fast forward ten years, I was working with a client whose sister was pregnant with twins. During the reading, Spirit was showing me my former professor and her twin babies. After more questioning with Spirit, I came to understand that Spirit was using that Life Story as a key to point out that the same thing is happening to my client's life. It was not my favorite message to relay from Spirit but they were prepared.

A few weeks later, my client reached out to me expressing her gratitude. She informed her sister and they had gone in for regular testing and she asked if there was a test to find that information out. It was determined that in fact one of the twins had not grown a brain fully. This message from Spirit assisted the family in grieving and understanding that Spirit is with us at all times, loving us through every life experience.

FALLING GRAM

My husband and I went to grade school together. One day, he jumped off stairs to high five a sign. When he came down, he braced himself on the cement ground and broke both his wrists. One hand had a clean break, the other hand did not and his arm was cast in particular way. The shattered wrist would take more time to heal. Spirit saw I would remember this because not every day does this happen to someone I love.

Fast forward several years, and Spirit used this life story to help me help my Gram. My Gram was getting older and was starting to fall down a lot. Spirit was showing me over and over Sean falling when he was a child and breaking his arms. After a week of this memory on repeat, I made it my intention to teach Gram how to fall safely. (Tuck your chin, think about spaghetti noodle and how they are flimsy and make your whole body like that.)

Gram called one day and said she fell. I was about to check on her but she told me she was fine. She did what I showed her to do. At the last minute she pulled her arms in to support her neck and so she wouldn't break her arms. The doctor said upon her checkup that she was smart to do that because a break would have not just meant her arms but her foot and hip as well.

BLUE ENVELOPES

After college, I was working for an advertising company. I had been working there a few years and I knew it was time for me to find a new job. Spirit was showing me it was time to work at a different company. During my daily meditation, I asked Spirit to show me a sign that would confirm that my next job was right for me in this journey.

A few weeks had gone by and I was in the middle of a wonderful dream. I was in this dream that was set in an office with long hallways. I saw all these different people and some were holding these large blue envelopes. The energy was calming and exciting. The people were happy and excited to see me. As I walked down the hall, I noticed all the different faces and how bright the light was shining on all these blues envelopes. I journaled about my dream and all the details. I shared the story with my husband over breakfast.

The recruiting agency that I was working with had me interview over the phone for a temporary job. The company was a large company who was known to hire on temporary workers but was hard to land a job interview with. I was thrilled. I heard back from the recruiter that I had the temporary job and I would start the next day.

Upon arriving for my first day at this large company, I was ready to work. As I was walking to my new desk, we turned the corner and it was as if I was walking in my dream from a few days ago; there were blue envelopes in workers' hands all the way down this long hallway. All the people from my dream were the same people I was meeting in real life and each person had a blue envelope – the same as the dream.

When I returned home from my first day, I shared with Sean, my husband, that my dream came true with the blue envelopes. Spirit was showing me that this is where I was to be working. I was a temporary hire and needed to make that permanent. The next day, I was asked to interview for keeping the job permanently. Little did I know that this job would give me the opportunity to move across the country and live in California. That story is for another time.

When Spirit informs you that they will use your Life Stories (key) to send a message, it is powerful. Spirit introduces the data patterns over and over until you pick up the message. This is a great example to use your mind palace to store these Spirit experiences for your reference and all the keys you create with Spirit. Along with all the keys, they are forever growing, as you are.

7

THE ONE WITH SPIRIT'S MIND AND BODY TRAINING

"Education is not the learning of facts, but the training of the mind to think."

— ALBERT EINSTEIN

MIND BODY REACTION FACTION

Like Mr. Einstein said, we are in the midst of training your mind to use your together with your body to communicate with Spirit. The Mind Body Reaction Faction is when your sense of reality is altered because you are communicating with energy in a whole new way – as a medium. Also, it's when you receive Spirit messages from your body and mind at the same time. All your senses slow down and reality is in slow motion.

Your body is communicating to your mind that you have a message from Spirit. Also, your mind will tell your body you have a message from Spirit. When this happens, time will slow for you and you are able to observe.

Observe your environment to seek the messages that are speaking to you or pulling your focus. Use your senses to gather the data. The keys we have created – Spirit's Love, Intention, Logic, Dream and Life Stories – will set you up for success in communicating with Spirit.

We use our keys to set our minds up for Spirit's love and messages. When our environment is being altered, our breath is the first way to understanding. Our meditations and breathing are a few ways to raise our minds to the appropriate vibration level to communicate with Spirit. We need to prime our bodies to get our minds to connect with Spirit. Sometimes Spirit will thrust us into an experience and you find you are in the Mind Body Reaction Faction. When that is done, Spirit is showing us that you can raise your vibration faster than before. Allow Spirit to guide your energy to that higher level. Your mind, body, and spirit are all intertwined. They are constantly giving each other messages to help you understand your environment around you.

Why is the Mind Body Reaction Faction happening? Spirit got your attention and the energy love flow is strong between you both. You have worked hard listening and asking questions to Spirit. Spirit wants to teach you through experiences and also to check in with your body often so that you understand when the Mind Body Reaction Faction occurs. What better way than to slow the environment to communicate to with you.

Remember that the breath is the quickest way to understanding the message deeper from Spirit. When this started for me, I started meditating in my mind palace with Spirit to understand what is being asked of me. This is when you are able to have Spirit give you a message through your mind and body at the same time, with both senses giving information together. You are learning to multi-task messages from Spirit. Which way the information comes to you first does not matter. That you received both is what is important.

HOW WILL YOU KNOW?

Trust me. Your environment will feel completely different. Like if you have ever visited the beach, there is the ocean water and its mist is everywhere. The feeling is like that. There is mist there that I can't really see but I feel it in the air. You will feel a comfortable but different energy that you take notice of. Like seeing a beautiful flower, you take notice.

SMART BODY

The body houses all of this information so we need to keep it in shape so the communication with Spirit is accurate. Being in sync with your body and its flow is helpful. If we don't know what is going on with our bodies, how is Spirit going to know how to communicate? For example, my left shoulder hurts in a particular way – I know my shoulder feels pain-free – that is not my energy at all. If my left shoulder was already in pain, Spirit would not use my hurt shoulder to give me a message. My body would not be healthy for receiving a message. Since you are in alignment with your body, Spirit feels that, as well and knows.

SMART MIND

When you want to receive further information from Spirit, an easy way is to ask with yes or no questions. Keep them simple – no gray areas. When speaking to Spirit, visualize a simple question you would ask a five-year-old. A five-year-old is pretty good at answering yes or no questions. This simple communication is needed with Spirit. Why do they need to speak that simply? Because life is complex and communication lines get crossed. When you start slow, the bond gets strong faster than you understand.

How do you understand if you receive a yes or a no from Spirit? How do you want to get a yes communicated to you? Through our imaginations and communication with Spirit. Each of us is different and we receive and share information differently. Different people are different. For example, my friend Abby loves the smell of toasted sesame seeds. She asked Spirit if the answer is yes, I want to smell toasted sesame seeds. If the answer was no, she wanted to see a large red X in her mind. Abby took a breath asked her question then took another breathe and smelled toasted sesame seeds. (The question she asked was if she should let me put this story in my book.)

Our imaginations are limitless, so find your yes and no with Spirit and keep it so it is easier with each experience. For myself, I like to spice it up and keep myself on my toes. If there is a particularly fun situation, then I'll switch my yes to a warm breeze and sometimes others around me feel it. One thing that I want to make clear is that you have a bond with Spirit – your own special bond – and you can use any of your senses to get a yes or a no. It's your language to create together and there is no wrong way to do this.

If you are unsure of your yes or no, then ask the same question again with the same designees. Understanding and having the courage to do this is rewarding and Spirit, knowing you want to get the clearest message, makes the vibration stronger. If you are still unsure of the answer from Spirit, take a breath and center yourself. Then kindly ask Spirit to literally spell it out for you in your mind or give you a sign right now, for you, in your time, in your space and in your language. Be silent and breathe. Spirit answers.

I HEARD IT

I was at my Gram's house finishing up planting her flower bed. There were a few flowers left over and I brought them inside. We were going to bring flowers to the cemetery for my grandpa Bill. I gathered all the flowers left over then added some tulips and lilacs. His flowers were going to be gorgeous.

I was beginning to experience the mind reaction faction. My Gram was talking and it was in slow motion. Sean was walking across the lawn and I thought he was impersonating the Bill Murray slow walk. Everything slowed down. I had a message from Spirit from my mind and it was to bring more flowers, more flowers. Then my body message came through at the same time but I can only type one sentence at a time to tell you. My left arm felt as if I was carrying a large water jug. I felt an instant pull and my arm and leg wet indicating there was a water jug in my hand. I then wanted to verify if I was to bring water and more flowers.

I asked – "Spirit, do you want me to bring more flowers and water to the grave?" I took a breath and was quiet until I heard the TV turn on by itself and say yes. I jumped because the TV was off and no one was in the room. Thank you to Spirit. I heard your message.

When we arrived at the cemetery, I placed the flowers on grandpa's grave. I thought he would show up like he used to, leaning up against the tree, smoking a cigarette. I didn't see him that day. What I did see beyond the tree was gravestone whose flowers were turned into mulch by the garden artists also known as gardeners. After we said our prayers and placed the flowers, Gram and I looked at each other and said the extra flowers are for them. There were two graves that we put flowers on and a warm breeze fell over our skin after our prayer at their graves. My Gram had me bring a large water jug. It was heavy in my left arm.

PSYCHIC KEY

You raised your vibration to be open to communication to Spirit. Your bond is strong. You understand the Mind Body Reaction Faction. Spirit wants to communicate more with a twist. You connected with Spirit to get a fuller communication picture. All mediums are psychics. Not all psychics are mediums. A psychic means "of or relating to the human soul or mind" according to dictionary.com. Psychics are specifically given a special intuitive gift to read the energy imprints from people, places, and things. They have the ability to read the energy from the past, present, and future as well. Psychic messages are received not from loved ones on the other side. Mediums raise their vibration to elevate to connect from the other side. Psychics do not have that ability.

GIFTING FROM SPIRIT

I had guitar lessons with a great teacher. I scheduled my first lesson for the following week. It couldn't get here fast enough. Finally, next week arrives, and I'm ready to leave for my lesson. I get a psychic message. It doesn't make sense so I check with Spirit. I was told to listen.

The psychic message was to bring a gaming lanyard to your new guitar teacher. I was gifted two new gaming lanyards the day before. I immediately acted like a little kid and said those are mine. Then I realized this wasn't about me. It was about my teacher receiving this lanyard, my gaming one, as a gift. Time to surrender to Spirit's love and step out of the way. After all, I had two and I could share.

I was off to my guitar lesson. I greeted my teacher and told him I had a gift. He was shocked. I said if you don't like it won't hurt my feelings, I'll take it back no problem. Now I piqued his curiosity and he was intrigued by this gift. I'll finish this story but first let me tell you about stepping aside for messages.

STEP ASIDE

We need to be able to tell our minds and bodies to step aside so our soul can connect with Spirit. This means everything that you are thinking. All that overwhelms you. Place it in a suitcase, put it outside the door, and step aside into Spirit's love and receive the message. When developing this step, I would often take a step and tell myself to step aside for Spirit and love to come through with a message. By doing this repetitive action, it has been easier and better.

The message you receive has nothing to do with you and what current events are going on in your life. It is about being in service to Spirit and his love. The detailed message you receive psychically will not make sense to you because it is not for you. Accept all of the information with no judgment and it will make sense to the person you need to help. Back to the guitar lesson story.

When I was at my guitar lesson, I gifted my gaming lanyard to my teacher and his face lit up. With a grin like a Cheshire cat he said, "Oh wow … how did you know I needed one? This morning, on my way to class, mine broke and my keys fell everywhere and it sucked. My friends laughed." He thanked me. Then after further review of what picture was on the lanyard, he screamed. The lanyard was for his favorite video game he was playing at the time. He looked at me and said, "How did you know?" I told him that I am a psychic medium and I was told you needed a new one. What was so humbling was his favorite video game lanyard made him happy. I was grateful for the Spirit interaction.

It's been years and I haven't thought about that lanyard since I gave it to him. That action used my mind, body, and spirit to help another soul. To this day, and it has been several years, he still brings up the day I gifted him his favorite gaming lanyard.

The complexities of using the body, mind, and spirit as symbols for communication is deep. For meditation's sake and for safety, keep the meditations going. This will help for knowing you, knowing your guides, knowing spirit intertwines body, mind, and spirit to help. Keep asking Spirit questions.

8

THE ONE WITH SPIRIT PATTERNS

"It's all in the mind."

— GEORGE HARRISON

By using all the keys created to understanding your medium gifts, it reveals the keys that are the data pattern collectors. These keys bring the definitions to your experiences with Spirit. When we work with Spirit in a disciplined way, the communications are easy. When you get a new dog, first you decide to get a dog. What type of dog? How big? How do we want to train the dog? The first trick to train is sit. You do this every day, because we want the dog to sit on command and respond. It takes time, patience, and repetition. When building your bond with Spirit, take your time and go slow. Meditate and communicate with Spirit daily, first thing when you wake up. Take just five minutes in the morning to just say hello. You will feel a change and Spirit's presence on a higher vibration.

You may have never meditated daily or in this way

before – it is new. It all comes back to language. The language you have with yourself is then related to Spirit. We need to be clear with our intentions of connecting. Repetitive communication with Spirit helps. A baseball player learns how to hit every ball a pitcher sends their way. There are so many types of pitches. The batter needs to know how to interact with the ball and not be shy. We need to strengthen how we use our keys to receive the clear message.

To strengthen the language, journaling helps, calling it out when it happens helps. Spirit doesn't have to be sensory appearing near you to know you said something out loud. If you say it in your head, they will hear it. How? You had the intention to speak to them.

BUILD UP YOUR MIND PALACE

This is the part of mind palace building that is wonderful. If you keep repeating the intentions, the subconscious mind will be in sync with you. If you keep repeating the communication daily with Spirit, you will have endless use of your mind with housing all the data from your experiences. If you make the intention for the mind to retain this information and bring it to you, it is never lost. All the keys retained in your mind palace will grow, as you do with Spirit.

Processing all this information can be overwhelming. Sometimes you have to tell Spirit to slow down more. We are human after all. Some Spirit guides have been human and understand. Other Spirit guides have never journeyed to the earth plane and don't quite understand. We have to remind them we are human and our feelings and processing are in a different reality.

The breath is key to control your mind-body-spirit so

you are knowing and fearing cannot flood your space. Often movies or TV – and most certainly folklore – has created some of the best scary experiences to witness. It is true though. Once you master your control of fear with your breath, you have just opened a new level to vibration. Spirit will see you advance and take you to the places in your imagination that can become your reality. Then you question yourself all over again.

PINK BELUGA

I was younger than fifteen years old and I had a vision that there was a pink beluga whale with a scar across its side that wanted to say hi to me. I never had an animal want to say hi to me before, but I was loving this and thinking, "Wow! I have a great imagination. A pink beluga whale is making me smile." Now, I had no idea what a beluga whale looked like but I did know that they were probably not pink. When you think whale, I think blue or gray. I assumed it would be gray. I went about my day, and made sure I journaled about it, as it was out of the ordinary.

Two weeks later on a field trip to the zoo they had a special visitor – a pink beluga whale. WHAAAAAT? It was the same pink whale I saw in my vision with the same scar across its side. I immediately started shaking in my shoes and all the hair on my neck stood up. I was taken aback. I was not aware that Spirit created. This was true. Pink Whales? I started laughing because that was the moment I realized I needed to open my imagination like never before because you will get messages that are just fun. You may find out why they came to you in a minute, or five years, or over decades. Some say you may understand yourself better after you transition to grace. I take time to use my imagination every chance I get with Spirit. It is another way to bond stronger.

I was also happy I journaled about it because I was able to go back and understand Spirit on a new way. Having fun with Spirit can bring joy. That pink whale was so cute and that is checked off my bucket list.

A HOLY VISIT

My Gram wanted me to go with her to visit her friend and I didn't want to. I told her there were too many people there and I didn't want to be crowded. She told me there would not be anyone there because she lived alone. That is why we were visiting her. I would not budge and told her I would not go the next day. I told her, "No, she has a whole house full of people there because I saw it last night when I was praying in Spirit 's lap."

Our visit didn't happen because of me. My Gram told me she called her friend and found out that her relative came to town and brought his whole family to surprise her. The whole house would have been packed. If we would have gone to the house at the original time, we all would have arrived at the same time, and it would not have been good for my Gram's friend. She is not a fan of surprises.

I loved my Gram's friend. I had been to her house several times. It was normal for us to go to the house and visit for a short time. It was out of the ordinary for me to keep pushing my Gram. That is not something I did. I was lucky my Gram listened to me. It was then I realized that I saw things before other people knew they were going to happen. How was this? Who could do this? Never stop asking the questions – to Spirit? To me? To a teacher? To someone who has had wonderful life experiences of helping others, through Spirit and his love. We sometimes help people before they know it. That can throw people for a curve. This is another layer of your medium gifts – previewing the future. A generalized term is predictions. I don't like that because of the meaning it has taken on. This is part of your psychic ability as a medium. You can view the soul's whole timeline with a few discretions.

Again with practice, you will use your senses to feel it this gift is a key. The Psychic Key is one to add to your mind palace. The psychic ability takes the form of many communications.

Sometimes I see a calendar and am shown a specific date for a person. Or I'm asked how long something will last. This is a great time to use your imagination to create with Spirit. Anything goes that comes from a place of love of Spirit.

Now if I need to ask Spirit about time, I gently remind them of my time and my space but they are not that far from us – just they don't have time. Setting up symbols for time and calendar time is a fantastic key to cultivate the Time Key.

Time, as in a twenty-four-hour period, is a fantastic symbol to have with Spirit. In your meditation, you will have the process to understand how you want the clock to be used, what it means for the family lineage line: clean clock, messy clock, what does the time tell you.

Spirit needs to know what your definitions of time are and what you want to know using time clocks. Are you trained in the military time? Do twenty-four-hour clock times make sense in your head?

This is similar to using a calendar. What does the person need to know about calendar time that will help them at this time? Who do I need to tell? Is there a change in that time of year? Then do the meditation for the calendar and receive the message. Go through your questions to Spirit. It will all happen and come together with practice. I know it sounds like you ask and just get an answer. This is skill that takes a lot of discipline and nurturing. The earlier you start, the easier it is.

You are in control of what and how you get your information. You need to work with Spirit to tell them.

We are all born with intuition. It is a muscle we need to flex but most of us outgrow it or it doesn't get nurtured. The intuition muscle is not used. There have to be several times in your life when someone said I was not feeling that. I didn't want to go there or I had a bad feeling. That is our intuition in a form helping us decide what we want and don't want in our lives.

The keys you acquired are going to show up to you through patterns. What you do with that data is up to you. For myself, I do not like spirits scaring me. If you just appear in my face – goodbye. We need boundaries with our mind palaces.

If I didn't have boundaries, I would not have a life. There are so many spirits that love talking to their loved ones. They hear us think about them. Sing about them. Write poems about them. Write music about them. Or when we smile when thinking of them. The life on the other side wants to interact with us – we just sometimes miss the communication. You have missed it or you wouldn't be reading this book right now and thinking of other people who would benefit from reading this book.

When you have boundaries, this radiates through the world. I helped a friend and his family member with a heart-loving situation. I was able to grant my friend's family member one of his last bucket lists wishes. No, it wasn't getting a reading from me. Although I do like what you are thinking. The person was so excited to have that experiences. It was being in Spirit's loving grace.

After years, my friend's family member had transitioned and would come and visit me. This person wanted to give my friend messages. I was so excited at first to do it, so I was calling at all times of the night, and during work hours. I thought well, it must be important. It was they wanted to be reminded they were loved. I did have to have a strong boundary because it was becoming all day, every day. I had to have my life back. It was a bit extreme. I know he was helping me have boundaries with Spirit because if I didn't master that, my health would be at risk and I wouldn't have a life.

State your boundary. If Spirit doesn't listen, they need to leave. It is that simple. You are talking to a four-year-old and you need to be clear. There can't be ifs, thens, or buts. Your health is too precious to do that.

I would have spirits smooshed up against the window wherever I lived. They were waiting for me to meditate so they could come inside when I meditated. I learned the hard way and boy did that scare me.

I thought I was being mean by excluding spirits. (Not doing this now Spirit.) I invited them all in at one time. I was knocked on my ass. I felt like everyone during the Chicago Cubs winning the pennant were coming at me at one time and saying, "Cubs win! Yeah!"

It was the scariest experience. Do not make that mistake and be lax in your boundaries. This is how people get hurt and low energy runs chaos in your life.

I have a no tolerance policy. I enforce it and I am strict. My life depends on it. How is that? Well, Spirit has endless energy and never needs to sleep. I need to participate in my life. There is a toll any job has on the body. It is no different for mediums. We are moving energy just like you.

We just happen to read the energy and it takes up a lot of mine to do so.

You will know when your boundaries are soft because chaos starts and your messages are not clear and it is difficult to clean up when you are not aware of it. How to have good boundaries: list out for Spirit how you want to talk and how you will listen.

I do not want to hear you outside of my head.

You do not come in my home or car without my permission. (Yeah, I had a spirit come and thank me for sharing their message and I thought a deer was heading through my passenger window.) That's not a cool feeling.

It wasn't the spirits' fault. They were new on the other side and excited that they could find me and give me a message of thanks. I understood why it happened the way it did. I needed to make a boundary for my car and how spirits can come and thank me.

After I made my boundaries, I state them in my intentions when working with Spirit and I have never had that happen to me again. There is so much to share. I'm so glad you are open to this. When you open your mind, the peace that comes with it feels amazing.

I know you are thinking more information to understand and store. That is what your mind palace is for. This is the place where all new things can go. Now if you feel overwhelmed, don't worry. Spirit will not let you down.

The last part of data patterns to learn from Spirit is about your life. What are your life data patterns? If you realized that your big life data pattern has the main pattern ingrained of Spirit's love. Winner winner chicken dinner. Love is the answer. How are you using love to communicate with Spirit? When you use love, miracles happen. They are heard and answered.

One day, I was praying for myself to not be hurt physically. I just did not want it. I felt like it was bad. I asked Spirit to keep me healthy. For seven days straight, I prayed for health for myself. Two days after my sixteenth birthday, I was in a car accident. The last thought I had before the truck crash into us was, "Dear God, please help me. Thanks." I flat-lined three times.

My heart stopped beating five times in my life and I remember every time. Having been on the other side, you pick up some wisdom and share it. I joke now that Spirit wasn't ready for me and I got kicked out of heaven.

Every time I was so happy not to have to breathe. It is so hard for me to do. Now I understand why my breath is so important.

What is it like on the other side? It was different each time. What brought me back to my body? Love. There was more work for me to do here and I was told I had the keys to share it with whoever wanted to learn. I am sharing my seven keys to Spirit Communication.

Unlocking your fear of the other side and knowing your loved ones are just a shout away is comforting. I heard my Gram praying the rosary when she found out I was in a car accident. Then I traveled to San Diego where her sister was praying the rosary with her. I found that out a year after the car accident, as I had a long recovery and to this day, have issues from that accident. I am here and I am alive and death is part of life. We are not getting out of this life alive, that is for sure.

In the death I experienced, there was no grim reaper. I asked where he was and they didn't know what I was talking about. I thought don't you people know everything up here. I then asked if they could hear me and they could. It was funny to me.

On the other side, I heard loved ones I know pray for me. Yes, we hear it. People who are taking their last breath hear you say, "I love you." That "I love you" cocoons them in your grace. If you have no clue what to do for a loved one who is dying, tell them how much you love them. Remind them how much love you have for them. Remind them of the experiences you have with them and how that love made you better. Tell that person your favorite song that reminds them of you because they love you. The love is what is going to help them be at grace point.

The grace point is the moment prior to the soul leaving the body. That is what I called it when I saw my consciousness or soul leave my body.

Why we don't feel our loved ones after they die? Our loved ones are getting used to being outside of the human form. Their mind needs to download all the soul experiences. Each soul has its own integration back to Spirit.

9

THE ONE WITH THE SPIRIT GUIDES YOU TO YOUR GIFTS OF SERVICE

"All your life, you will be faced with a choice. You can choose love or hate ... I choose love."

— JOHNNY CASH

I was looking over the hill at the cemetery with my Gram. I saw the trees waving in the gorgeous soul's lawn. You could smell all the flowers that are placed on the graves. There's a peaceful wave of love that you could feel there.

I looked at my Gram and thought one day I will bring flowers to you and look at the same trees but all alone. You and Grandpa Bill will be so happy because you miss him so dearly. I loved watching your blue eyes flicker when you mentioned him. It was not a lot because you would cry. I know he never left you, but you never were able to see him. I know you felt him because you would talk in your sleep to him when I would sleep over. I just thought my buddy was being nice to you and whispering sweet kind words to you. What I realized now is he was telling you how beautiful you are and how much he loves you.

I would see my Grandpa Bill around my Gram every time I was with her. It didn't matter where we went or who we were with. He was there. In my teenage years, I was scared of him because I didn't know what was going on. Ghost – I didn't know I was allowed to believe in that. Once I found out who he was, it was easier to see him in spirit form.

In that moment, I realized this is what being in service of Spirit's love is like. I was helping both of them. Do I know all the details of how, where, when, and what I helped them with? No. A lot of those details are none of my business. What is my business is my intention and my action with love to assist them. Love and support.

Yes, we help the other side. The loved ones we have on the other side keep the same personality from the earth plane. There may be some personalities that grow but the majority remain the same. If Uncle Bobby loved mint chocolate chips, then he will love it on the other side. This is why understanding what your key gifts are telling you about you and the other side matters. It also helps you expand those gifts.

I knew my Grandpa Bill wasn't visiting me every day. He was surrounding the love of his life with love. I knew he needed my help but what that help was, I needed to unlock. This is a perfect example of a spirit wanting to build a relationship with you because they are attracted to your vibration; it's like you both have the same taste in energy. There is a law of attraction – like attracts like. What we put out we are already getting back. The Be In The Love Key is an exercise to build your specific spiritual relationship muscle. In this moment, I realized I needed to be of service to my grandpa. The clear seeing is what my gifts were telling me I was most receptive to, in building my relationship. This was the door opening to nurturing this gift and learning from what it will mean to me and to you, Grandpa Bill, and Gram. I am not the only one who will feel the consequences of my choice to engage in nurturing this relationship.

This is like a new friend. You take time to meet the person. Set up talking times. If it goes well, you meet for coffee. Then after coffee, then meet for lunch, and so on and so on. You carve out time in your life to establish a friendship with a new person. This is the same with Spirit, only you hang out with them in a few different ways.

The most important way to hang out and hear Spirit is to have concentration. Concentration will give your energy and Spirit's energy the time to meet and greet. You will begin to understand if you are in the right place and time for concentrating, and if it is a good time for you proceed with Spirit communication. Are you open to receiving messages right now? I know when I'm trimming my dog's face, I don't want to speak to Spirit at that time.

MEDITATION

Take Spirit for a walk and have a conversation. Sharing information with Spirit is a form of meditation. Writing in a journal is a form of meditation.

You create a pattern just like you would with a new friend. It is the same with Spirit.

Then Grandpa Bill came to me in a different form: audio in my dreams. I've had dreams about him prior, but he never spoke. We heard each other, but our mouths did not move. It was clear as if we were communicating.

The audio in my dream was amazing. It was like the

best stereo I've ever heard. It got my attention, which I later realized was important.

The first time I had clear audio in a dream I was just about to graduate college. I asked myself, "Did that happen? Did I have that experience with my mind? Well, you are thinking it; imagination or not, you dreamt it." It's so surreal. My body feels like it's in a state of sleep and tingly all across my skin. Is that ectoplasm? Dan Akroyd flashes in my mind from *Ghostbusters* as he explains what ectoplasm is. Yup … yes … I decide it is.

The first audio dream is different from the second one. I immediately compared and contrasted. The first one is darker. The light comes from above and reminds me of an eighties cop-show where they interrogate criminals and shine a bright light from above. I looked at the light then I put my head down and saw a beautiful roulette wheel of gold, black, and red – deep, rich colors that automatically relaxed you into a comfortable breath. There is a lush green table where bets are placed except there is no grid for placed bets. A Salvador Dali melting clock was on the left. It had the same gold as the roulette wheel. It showed the time: two o'clock.

"What does it mean? Is it important because I can't take my eyes off of it?" I asked, its gold glistening from the light above. I ask out loud – "What does two o'clock mean?" My answer comes from two college friends popping their heads in and, in an intoxicating language slur, "Mumble and mumble it means 2:00 a.m." They repeated, "It means 2:00 a.m." I look to my left and get verification from Sean. Sean nodded as if to verify the truth. "Truth of what?" I thought. I got my answer from my Grandpa Bill when he appeared in a shadow outline. He said, "She will die at 2:00 a.m. It's up to you if you want to be present for it. It's your choice. Not hers. Not mine. Not Sean's. Yours."

The second dream started with a soft glow of morning light – the feeling of waking up before the world has woken and your thoughts are the first of the day in the world. Taking a deep breath. Just gorgeous and I looked around in this soft glow. Majestic comes to mind. I looked left and heard the sound of my Grandpa Bill saying out loud,

"Brennie, I don't know how to tell you but you need to be counseled and informed of a heart-rending life experience you are going to have. You are not directly affected but you do feel the consequences and are affected by that. You need to help her. Take her to the doctor and check in on her as much as you can. There's no need to tell you the when because that hasn't been decided. What I can tell you is the season of year it will happen to help you prepare. You need to get your mind, body, and spirit ready. Do you understand? You didn't die to not be ready for this. Meditate your mind so your body will follow and process. Your spirit will – that will take the rest of your life but you will be supported. Are you ready for the information?"

I paused.

I said, "No, once you tell me I will know and that begins the change in my life. So, no, I'm good." He said, "It doesn't work like that." All I felt was love. Every moment in my life filled with that love shooting at me. There are no more words to describe it. The hush of love feeling gets softer and I heard my Grandpa Bill say, "She will have a stroke on Christmas. It will be the beginning of her transition." He repeated, "Her transition." Then like a vacuum, all of the soft light filled with love vanished in my single breath of waking up.

Every Christmas I waited. Three years went by and nothing.

The last message hit me like a log dropped on the fire to keep it going. Breathing hurt. Seeing the picture hurt.

Hearing the words he told me hurt. Seeing my life before the hurt. Knowing my life after would hurt. How will Spirit, my Spirit, the one who sent me angels to bring me back to life want me to feel this pain? Who was going to have a stroke? I knew it was someone close and someone special. But then I denounced my dreams. This is too weird to happen. I asked, "Who does this happen too? Who?" My answer was me.

I was floating. This beautiful warm white color washed over every area I looked at. I was out of breath. Stairs – why would I climb all these stairs? Climbing to what seemed to feel like my future. Climbing to happiness.

I saw the living room, the kitchen, laundry room off the kitchen, bathroom, and last, the bedroom. It was gorgeous. I saw myself in the bedroom with oak furniture. There was a forest green comforter on my bed. I looked to my left and see my husband, Sean, lying next to me. I look right. The headboard is covering up the windows in the room. This shimmering white light looks like a door to heaven.

"Heaven is at my door, cool," I thought. I saw the cream-colored carpet with two big shoes. Filling those shoes was Grandpa Bill.

"Hi, look around, Brennie, see what I am showing you. Look at every detail. Choices have been made and I can give you more information. I have counseled you as much as possible. See the colors. See the man next to you. Feel his energy. Feel his love."

I heed his message and do what he instructed. I take in every detail. I tell myself pay attention to all your senses – this will help you. I see the furniture, the green comforter, and the brown-haired man. The unconditional loving man and I know he is Sean.

Grandpa said, "This is where you will be. This is how your furniture will be displayed. This is my last message for your mind, body, and spirit to prepare for her death. I have given you five years' time to prepare. Know that I will be there and you at this time. Brennie, remember this dream and tell Sean about it."

I woke up from the dream from Grandpa Bill and the phone rang. I picked it up and it was confirmed. All my dreams came to fruition. She died.

My Gram died. She continues to love me and I love her. I can't go into much more otherwise I won't be able to finish writing.

I didn't remember a single dream until after she was gone. (I call that medium amnesia.) Gram died from the results of a stroke that started on Christmas in 1999. She died at 2:00 a.m. When she transitioned, I was sleeping under the forest green comforter with my husband Sean in the oak decorated apartment.

The last dream of this life experience was from my Gram. She told me not to remember her death because it was only a small part of her life. "Remember my life span – it was bigger. Give me a bear hug, Brennie."

This specific interaction spanned over the course of five years – from the first dream from Grandpa Bill to the last with Gram. To set up and to be open to hear about the dreams took ten years of working with my grandpa. I was a teenager. No one was going to tell me what to do, so I took the longer road to get there. I hope you take the enlightened path – it is way more fun.

I learned a lot from this experience that has carried over the course of time. There were three souls and numerous other souls that benefited from this experience. I benefited, my Grandpa Bill, my Gram and family, friends, and now you. The love that traveled from my grandparents to me and back was beautiful. I am so grateful for this experience but it was one of the most devastating experiences.

I thought to myself I got all this good information from my dreams. I can share it with people and we can pray and Gram will not die. I'm here to fix this situation. I was confused, and thought I had to fix her death. "I am stronger than Spirit and can manipulate death because of these detailed dreams." My plan was if I don't see her, we will not have our last conversation before her death. I procrastinated going to her house. I argued with my husband and he said to me. "Bren, you're special but you are not so special that your will for her to live will change the outcome of her life." Like Grandpa Bill said, "This is why I communicated to you, to help you both with the transition." It was that moment that I realized I wanted to be a (s)hero and that she wouldn't die.

I meditated long to setup my mind to be more disciplined. I told myself, "Think of an opened suitcase. Drop inside the suitcase all your worries, fears, angers, and grievances and close it. Put that suitcase aside, feel the fear drowned out by love." I asked Spirit to take the thought from my head (not wanting her to die) to my heart – guiding her soul with Spirit's love back home. That is what I did. I kicked and screamed but eventually found peace to give us three what we all needed. I understood the glory of life loved and felt the sadness that our physical earth relationship was transitioning.

Gram's death took me to places I didn't know the mind, body, and soul could go. My imagination grew. Faith grew, grief grew, love grew. The grief (I felt … I am human and have emotions too) left me unable to read for three weeks. It took a toll. After I was able to read again, it took me another ten years to feel her energy. It was just too raw.

You will have some souls that are like that; you have to

have boundaries. I just had too many feels from her transition. It is okay. That is where I am with my relationship with her. If I want it to grow, I need to nurture it. I'm not ready yet. I'm taking baby steps with her.

I am the one who is in control of communicating to me. I had a boundary with my Spirit guides. My Grandpa listened and gave me the messages in my dreams like I requested. It was easy to have a rapport with my Grandpa Bill because it was exciting and a new experience. When you have that kind of energy behind your intention, it makes a difference.

I have had a few dreams from my Gram. There have been some that have come true and some that have not. I understand that I have not built that muscle with her to have a higher accuracy.

This is a huge part. Not every Spirit who communicates with you has a problem for you to fix. Most times, they want you to tell their loved ones hello and they see what is going on in their lives. They just want to say hi or be acknowledged. Not every time you are communicated to do you have to help them.

BE IN THE LOVE KEY

This chapter signifies a great channel of love for what you and your heart would like to gift to the world. This is the Be in the Love Key, which is filled with action. I know you're thinking just love everybody and everything and we will all be fine. It doesn't work that way. Action from the heart needs to be taken for the Be in the Love Key. If you're stating hollow, "I love yous" to the Universe, Spirit knows and just drops it to the bottom of the ocean. There is no love vibration attached to carry to the phrase like that to a loved one or situation. The phrase "I love you" is one of your most powerful weapons. You know how powerful words are. You have been hurt by them. You have been overjoyed by them. You know the consequence of believing in the words and that is how you know the power of words.

I want you to think about love in a new way. I want you to think about Be(ing) in the Love as your full circle key. This is a large key because it unlocks everything, everywhere, for all time and space. There isn't a material object that hasn't been touched by love at some point in time. That is the same for you. You love yourself, friends, family, and animals. It carries you through the day.

The Be in the Love Key has many essential silos of importance. Instead of love just being this boring verb by itself ... let's pull it close and dust it off and think of it as a heart action verb. When using love as a heart action verb, get ready to watch all your miracle requests unfold. This process works and has helped me, protected me, warned me, and given me the ability to pick up my internal love power off the floor and use it.

What is the plan to fully use the Be in the Love Key? First, Spirit needs to know what is going on. This is why concentration and meditating are so important for mediums. It is connecting to Spirit, connecting to love, connecting to each other, connecting to self. When you have the know-how to use the Be in the Love Key, you understand that this is the only key that ties all keys together. This key, cultivated in your mind palace, will have everlasting energy. Love never ends. Love never gets lost. Love connects us all in the earthly plane or the ethereal plane. It is the automatic connection to God/ Spirit, The Great Spirit, Buddha, Source, Universal Love, Energy – so if we all have love in our heart, we are then all connected. Sending prayers, intentions, messages over the channel of love reaches all who have love in their heart. Nothing can stop it.

When I state, I love Sean (my husband), I have the thought and drop it down to my heart put my love energy on that sentence. I want you to feel that. You know it's true. It also reminded you of the souls you love. You just said in your head a list of people that you wished your love to them.

When you splash love into a situation, the waves of love we ride on are not full of fear. These waves ripple out to places we don't know, and places, and people we do know. The smallest Be in the Love Key heart action is a smile. Maybe someone needed that today.

We all need love. We are all involved in love. We make it. We share it. Now it's time to learn how to fill our intention with the Be in the Love Key. We asked what is the obstacle, person, place, or thing that needs the Be in the Love Key.

How do you fill your intention with love? This is where the meditation practice comes into play. Quiet the mind. See the situation. Walk into the situation. Acknowledge the pain or hurt. Then wrap that up in Spirit's perfect love. Spirit is already there, waiting to guide you through His love. Say, "I surround myself with Spirit and all His love. I pray for love to ease this situation and bring clarity to light for this time and space. Thank you, Spirit, for all of your love."

When your head is filled with fear and you can't shake I, walk over to the front door, open it, and give the fear to Spirit. This is a great example of how to use the Be in the Love Key. You are telling fear to leave and allowing space for love.

Think of everyone you love and your favorite color. Flood your mind, body, and soul with love. So much love you can't even move in the room. Then I want you to visualize a root growing from that mind space. Follow that root growth all the way down to your heart. See that root cover that heart and make it glow. When your heart glows, then you know you are ready for asking for what you want Spirit's love to help you.

GRATITUDE

It's all about understanding love from a connective tool viewpoint. If we are all connected, we all feel each other on the love vibration. The Be in the Love Key connects all keys because we are all connected.

Do this: go for a walk in a park with trees in nature and love the place you go. No complaining on the way there or back from the walk. Every gaze your eye travels to on your walk, I want you to thank it. I see a tree. Thank you, tree. I see an ant. Thank you, ant. One the first half of your walk, do this step on repeat.

On your walk back home, just listen to your breathing as your heart beats. Smile and take in all of nature as you go home. What did you notice on your walk? Did the trees seem like they have more wind in them? Did the birds chirp a little louder? Did the dogs bark once to say hi? Did you see the colors seem a bit brighter? This ever so slight change is because nature heard your love and wanted to send it back to you.

There is a never-ending supply of love to support you in life and we have just begun to understand what it can do. These next generations – I'm so excited to see how they cultivate love into society to help others. There are times when we need to remind ourselves that yes, we are a creator of love and we are also a killer of love.

When you have filled your environment, body, mind,

and spirit with love, there is no room for fear. The Be in the Love Key dissolves fear with love. Fear will distort the course you are on; that is why concentration in meditation is important. The practice of mediumship is sacred and is deeply personal for you, your loved ones, and Spirit. This is not something to take lightly or think it is a fun game. This is why I want you to understand the Be in the Love Key.

Fighting fear is so daunting and energy sucking. I don't want you to fight fear. I want you to drown fear out with your love. You will have fears in mediumship. People will ask you questions that make you uncomfortable. This is another form of fear that will put you off. Disciplining the mind with meditation, daily, is so important.

Different people are different so meditation can be in many forms. Right before I wrote this paragraph' I listened to one of my favorite songs and it was great. That was my meditation to get myself aligned with love. Remember, this is a blueprint. I'm giving you foundational information to start a healthy, happy communication with Spirit.

Spirit wants you to master the one gift that you keep using over and over again. Spirit wants you to grow with this gift. Why is Spirit calling you to use your gift in that way? When you are in a vibration of Spirit love, how can that not feel good? Connecting to Spirit is connecting to love – something bigger than yourself. Also, you meet so many beautiful souls.

10

THE ONE WITH SPIRIT
UNLOCKING YOU

"As you think, you vibrate. As you vibrate, you attract."

— ABRAHAM-HICKS

All these keys are ways to communicate and house data regarding your Spirit experience. We add intention and the result is an action. Each key is different and each key will have layers to them. (Some keys will no longer work for your environment and then we will forge a new key. You'll learn that later.) These keys you have cultivated for yourself and others will unlock truths, wisdom, inspiration, compassion, and many more feels along your path. As you grow and develop, those skills under the keys get deeper. This is putting yourself aside and tapping in the soulful connection level.

After I put myself aside, I step into my soul level. When you tap into that level of yourself, your vibration of love is birthed. This is where Spirit fills you with all that your soul needs to live on earth to help yourself to help others.

We need this vessel of you to be in the best shape your body, mind, and soul can be for that given movement.

First, understand each key starts with a general definition and after time your relationship with Spirit grows and so does the definitions of your keys. For example, you love animals. Loving animals is a category to add each key. The keys are needed to form a foundation to communicate with Spirit but we are all different people. The recipe for key making comes with time and experience.

The key recipe is simple but the energy behind making a key is important to understand first. There is no starter kit of keys sets to purchase and hope they all work. Each key that is created needs utmost dedication, time, and reverence. There is a lot time and effort to construct them. Each key is used differently for each circumstance or experience you have. Just like our fingerprints, they are unique as the individual or soul we are connecting to.

Each of the keys will have a name and definition, and you will have more than one that you store in your mind palace. Each key will have several layers and or actions definitions for them. You are one person who will be interacting with several different souls. The keys are a great way to set yourself up to connect with Spirit.. Think of it like text messaging Spirit for support. Or instead of asking Siri, you ask Spirit. When you use your keys, Spirit knows what you are communicating because you have been mediating and well, Spirit is the creator of everything.

After each Spirit experience with a loved one or psychic information, add it to your mind palace. The mind palace houses all the data of souls you assisted that were in need of service. For example, when I say the color blue to you, what do you think of? The majority may think sky or ocean. There is a symbol you have for the color blue already. If sky or ocean was not what you thought of, that is okay. This is an additional symbol of the color blue. This is the same for keys. There are many definitions to them and this chapter will help you develop that skill.

KEY CULTIVATING

Main Recipe for making your keys is simple. This is a four-ingredient recipe. No baking, or boiling, required.

Key Making Recipe

CALL | Spirit
TO | Concentration in prayer
ACTION | Love
THANK YOU | Gratitude

One, we do all things through Spirit and all of His/Her love. This is our Call to Spirit. Two, we put ourselves aside, concentrate in prayer until we feel the Holy Spirit. Three, we think of all the love we have experienced, and put that in the key to create the action we need from this key. Four, we give gratitude for this entire experience, being open to new information from Spirit.

Let's get into the details about what all this means. Call Spirit to help you surrender your inhibitions so you may concentrate in prayer to put yourself aside so love may reign upon your path to guide you with words or actions. Spirit lifts our vibration to meet the messages we can receive. Spirit's love is everywhere and a part of everything. It is in nature at its finest. How your senses interpret Spirit there is love.

To see all this – love all the time – can be overwhelming. That is why concentration in prayer is a daily exercise you already put in action. If you just said you don't, well, we just planted a seed for you to change your point of view. Come join us daily for our Spirit connection. You know you feel good afterward.

Concentration can start small. You don't have concentrate for an hour at a time. It can be a full minute if you like. Okay, let's cut it down even more. Let's do it right now for ten seconds. All I want you to think about is your breathe being the color blue on your inhalation and exhalation. Go, I'll count.

1, 2, 3, 4, 5, 6, 7, 8, 9, 10

The next time, add twenty. Until you can master a full minute, just practice. We will see these small habits have grand benefits along with your key learning experience.

Here's another example of concentration. You just bought a new shirt. You washed it and it is ready for its new home. "Where to put it?" You take a few seconds and ask yourself a few questions about the shirt. "When will I wear it? How often do I wear it? Does it need to hang up or be folded?" All these questions are a form of concentration. You want the best place for your shirt but it takes concentration to figure it out.

This is the same for molding your key to fit the experience in your life and to let your support system on the other side know this is the best way to communicate with me.

Concentration is directly connected to listening. If your mind is going and going, and then immediately you have no idea what is going on in your environment, then a recalibration is in order. Spirit has been giving you information. Listen from your inner self for Spirit. Listen, not with just your ears with all your senses. What is our body, mind, and soul revealing?

This is like riding a bike – it just gets easier over time. The easier it gets, the faster you can drop your intention into your heart and see the path to the miracle or have the patience to wait for the miracle to appear in your life. Have the knowing that you are in Spirit's love and will.

When we feel Spirit's love, it is felt down to the bone. There will be times when you have a chill that chiseled its way down your spine and made your skin have goose bumps. The feeling tells us to use love as an action. Love is the action of the soul. Love is the action from Spirit. Spirit is love and love is Spirit. Love reminds us we have no separation from Spirit. Love reminds us to ask for help .

These keys we stored in our mind palace will be updated, changed, added onto, or replaced with new. They are ever moving in miracles, just like you. They are also a way to have you focus on the message and how you are receiving it.

You are setting up your mind to connect with Spirit on a new level consistently. This takes time to call Spirit, time to concentrate, love, and gratitude. It is simple. We don't need to complicate anything with Spirit. Life is hard enough.

THE SEVEN SPIRIT COMMUNICATION KEYS

1. Key | Spirit's Love
2. Key | Intention
3. Key | Logic
4. Key | Dreams
5. Key | Life Stories
6. Key | Psychic
7. Key | Be in the Love

Key | Spirit's Love

The Spirit's Love Key you will call on for everything. No action should be taken by you unless this love is connected first. Spirit is love. Love is Spirit. The relationship love you have and believe you have is the main key. There are many reasons for this and the two main reasons I'll touch on.

Spirit's Love Key, one, is the energy state you can help yourself and to help others. Two, safety.

Key | Intention

The Intention Key is the foundational key. All questions are asked from a place of love. If you come from a place of fear, your communication is compromised. It is compromised because you replaced love with fear as your foundation.

Key | Logic

The Logic Key uses our common sense to understand what is happening in our experience with Spirit. It also dispels fear and scientific understanding is a reason. For example, you feel a warm breeze and you see the oven door is open. You used your common sense to locate the reason for the change in your environment. Using logic when communicating with Spirit is a pair used together for life.

Key | Dreams

The Dream Key has two definitions. One, a dream is a kind of meditation while our mind is communicating with Spirit. Two, is allowing your mind to follow thought to thought and after a short period of time, you realize you have not been in reality; you have been having a conversation with Spirit. Both kinds of dreams are two new ways for Spirit to communicate to you with a lot of information. Understanding our Spirit symbols in our dreams is another layer to add to our communication.

Key / Life Stories

The Life Stories Key uses our own specific life experiences to use as present day symbol of communication. Use your limitless imagination – because Spirit will.

Key / Psychic

The Psychic Key is understanding that you were given a special intuitive gift to read the energy imprints from people, places, and things that could be from the past, present, and/ or future.

Key / Be in the Love

The Be in the Love key is the key that directs us back to love and to holding it in our space. Being in the love and holding that energy is a gift from Spirit and takes practice and time. Think about a loved one and all the love you have for them. All that love is Spirit and that brings us back to Spirit's Love Key.

THE ONE WITH THE SPIRIT
RELATIONSHIP CHOICE

"Our deepest fear is that we are powerful beyond measure."

— MARIANNE WILLIAMSON

S pirit has reached out to you regarding your medium gifts and the choice has come to understand fully what this means. I want you to have the full spectrum of Spirit requirements for communicating.

ROUTINE

A daily routine is what is needed to keep your communication flow with Spirit. There may be days you don't want to do this at all. How would you tell Spirit that? Developing a consistent routine is most important. This is a connection and it needs to be nurtured daily. You have a busy life – how will this fit in? Do you want it to? Because sometimes, you may have your day planned and it does not go that way.

ON CALL

You have said to Spirit, "I am here please use me and help me to help others." If you don't have daily communication or routine, expect to be on call whenever they want to talk. Yes, when you have to go on vacation and the schedule is tight and you have 101 things to do before the taxi gets there or your friend drives you. They don't care. They feel your excitement and want to join in the fun. What you want another four hours of sleep before the kids wake up, Spirit wakes you and wants your attention. When you lack your routine, get ready for a wild experience that is not fun at all.

I lacked in my daily routine while I moved across the country in a job transfer. On my first day of work, I received a joke email and my computer speakers automatically turned the volume up full blast and played the most inappropriate phrase, "Hey, everybody I'm looking at porn." I looked at my new boss and asked if I was fired and she looked at me puzzled. There are no audio speakers for the computers or monitors for a message to play out loud. Spirit wanted me to know it was funny that I moved across the country. I was on call.

I was sitting in a conference room with C-suite executives discussing the best marketing strategy for our current movie. The CEO asked me, "What do you think the best strategy is, Bren?" Right after that question, when the room is silent, my brand-new smart phone notification sound plays Will Ferrell saying, in a Ron burgundy voice, "Whale's Vagina." Spirit thinks you are paying attention. I was on call.

BOUNDARIES CROSSED

Spirit will have no boundaries with you until you let them know. They see your whole soul and connecting with you at any time is easy for them. Spirit doesn't have time on their side. If you do not share that, tell Spirit you are sleeping – do not wake me up during the night to tell me a message. Or you could be driving and they just appear in your windshield.

I didn't have any boundaries when I first started because I had a distortion. I told myself I'm working with Spirit and I was welcoming everyone under the sun to speak with me. Would you invite everyone – and I mean everyone – to your bedroom every night before you go to bed? Well, that could be one of the things that happens. It's like you turned your social media status on and everyone on the internet wants to ask you one question at the same time. Then if the Spirit speaks in another language, it gets more confusing.

Do you want your Aunt Maggie popping up in the shower asking you about talking to Aunt Gladys today because it's her birthday and she wants to remind her of how much she sends her love and gives her kisses on the forehead? Where are the shower boundaries? Oh yeah, there are no boundaries unless you make them.

ENVIRONMENT

Understanding what exactly is going on in my environment is not always a walk in the park. I was losing a clear understanding of the energy in my environment. I didn't know where my energy began or ended or where Spirit's began or ended. I thought if this is the love vibration, then

I don't have to scan my environment, I don't have to be responsible for it.

Let me ask you this – do you drive in a motorized vehicle? Have you driven in a car, train, plane, bus, or truck? When in a vehicle, are you responsible for you? Are you responsible for how you drive or behave while in the vehicle? That is being responsible for your environment. You are not going to look at the road and see a big pot hole and drive right in it when there is a sign that has a detour that would keep you safe. This is the same for your environment. If you are not understanding the energy in your environment, it will lead you back to loose boundaries.

DREAMS

There will be times when you want to have a cool dream from a loved one so you may help, but what you get is something else. You may get dreams that make no sense and years later, it helps someone, but you were too late to share your dream and missed being of service of Spirit.

I lost of friend because of a dream. In my dream, I saw the fruition of her new relationship and she is so excited and she wants to have babies with this new man. She does marry him and get divorced and it leads her to having a rough time in her life. I just needed to tell her about the dream; I thought, "It's too big and she would tell you." I told my friend and she decided we are no longer friends. She was convinced I wanted her spotlight. (They never married; he left her for a job across the world.)

The dream you have about a massive shooting and people are screaming at you to help them and it feels so real like you are there and you cannot do anything – in this dream, you are paralyzed. You wake up from the dream and feel it was a nightmare, only to find out three hours later your dream was a teleplay of the newscast in the morning airing the story to the details of your dream. What do you do in that moment? What was that all for? What does Spirit want you to do with that? Do you want to be notified more when there are mass shootings?

MEDIUM HELPERS

There are souls on the other side that are attracted to your vibration, and your energy, and your personality. Some call them angels, lady friends, gentleman friends, angels, Spirit guides. We all have them throughout our life. Some mediums know their whole group of helpers. Some do not. Understanding that you have them in all areas of life is okay but it is difficult to establish a connection and then they change it up on you, once you get that connection. There is a revolving door of Spirit guides.

They come in all shapes and sizes. Use your imagination and that is how they come to help you. Choose an area of your life and there is one. If you don't know your guide, but other people do, it is off-putting and a bit frustrating. Every place I've lived, a neighbor describes one of my guides that hangs out in my front door. Where I am, my spirit guides are there. At a friend's house, new home, vacation hotel. Spirit guides are present. Over time, I have had so many neighbors suggest I receive a blessing by a priest. It has gotten funny, but it wasn't at first.

There are some spirit guides who think if they make you laugh, it will raise your vibration so you both can connect. Tickling your feet at night when you are sleeping is not cool or itching your toe when driving on the freeway is not fun. Or tickling your nose during the best part of the movie … not cool.

At the time, I was not a coffee drinker. I was saying my

prayers and getting ready to do my weekly medium exercises with a friend when I had the strongest taste of coffee in my mouth. I explained to my friend. She laughed and said, "Oh, that is Todd. He loved coffee and he was a good healer when he was on the earth plane. I asked him to say hi to you." I didn't like that taste of coffee but appreciated the hello.

EXPAND IMAGINATION

The experiences you have already had are incomparable to your future with Spirit. The use of your imagination – and growing it – is hard but so essential. Conditioning the human mind to expand your imagination to comprehend communicating with Spirit in more than one form is overwhelming to process. How do I do that when do I do that? Let go of expectations.

The pain of expanding your imagination means anything goes and how do you interpret that? You get to decide. To limit your language with Spirit will get boring. It would be like talking to a four-year-old the same way for the rest of your life. You expand your imagination; you need to know yourself pretty well and concentrate with Spirit. It takes time and energy.

BODY TOLL

The physical toll on the mind, body, and soul can be harsh. You are moving energy, which takes a lot of energy use. You jump from being startled if you don't daily meditate to connect with Spirit. It doesn't matter if you think you are "only" praying. That thought took energy. We get into a routine about praying – it is automatic – and three hours have gone by, and I haven't eaten lunch, walked the dogs, or had any water.

Body checking yourself is a must. Know what your aches and pains are. Because we are moving energy, getting and receiving messages from Spirit, hydration and eating healthy are a must. When you move energy like you do, your cells need to have good food. One time I was giving a reading to a client and I ate fried food before the reading. It was a bad choice and that's all I'm going to say about that.

Keeping the body vessel at best shape is setting up yourself to get the messages. If you have heartburn and you are not feeling well, and you think it's Bart from work having a heart attack, you are getting the wrong message. You ate bad food and you thought of Bart because you have to talk to him tomorrow at work first thing.

UNBALANCED MIND

An unbalanced mind creates an unbalanced ego. Being grounded and centered is a sure way to connect with Spirit. What I mean by this, is you are getting message after message. You are delivering those messages and they are strong, filled with love and compassion. You think you are on a roll, like at the blackjack table in Vegas. No, you are not Spirit-aligned, my friend.

This happens to every new person. When we are pushed, we talk ourselves out of this and feel the negative of trying to help. "I'm helping. I'm doing good. That's it, right there. I am." You are the message delivery service from Spirit and His love to that soul you are interacting with. You are important. What you need to check is that you are not the one with the message; Spirit is. You are not the one who saw, or felt – Spirit did, and gave you that message.

FRAUD

You give a message to a friend about their future significant other. You share the whole message. What you didn't do is check with your guides for accuracy on the message. You didn't tell but you saw that on her way to her friend's house, he asks her to pick up beer. She says yes and when she is at the store, she meets the man of her dreams and hits it off and falls in love.

She feels she is late and brushes off the guy in the store because at the party she is going to meet her man. Well, during the time she took contemplating talking to the guy at the store, the other guy at the party left with another girl and they get married. Your friend comes back to you and tells you and everyone you are a fraud.

BLOCKING

There is a time when Spirit will block your gifts. This is when you are using them to hurt others in any way, shape, or form. This often happens to mediums when they are young teenagers and then when you're, older it comes back. The times depend on the person, place, and circumstances. There are mediumship laws that Spirit does abide by. You will know because you will get no response from Spirit and you will not have your gifts any longer.

APPROPRIATE GIVING

We may think we are helping our loved one but we are helping ourselves. This use of Spiritual Gifts in what Spirit chooses is not appropriate or negative. What those general consequences are for karma. What we put out we get back immediately.

I wanted to do a meditation with my friend, Laura, and we were at the pool. It was nice and quiet. Well, a group of people were there and got loud. I asked for Spirit to move them as I wanted to give my friend a great meditation and exercise. My prayer was answered and I was able to have a fantastic time and my friend learned a great deal from the exercise we did. When I went to get my massage, it was horrible. I was inconvenienced by sharing space with others and that inconvenience gave me the worst massage of my life. He non-stopped talked throughout the massage.

PROFESSIONAL

After reading this book, you do not automatically become a professional medium. Just like any athlete, training and exercise must be done consistently. You will be challenged about your profession.

I was invited to a social event and I was excited. It was about networking for young business women. The party is good energy. I was asked what I did for a living. I said I'm a medium. The person looked right at me and said I don't believe in that. I remained professional and said I never asked you to believe me. It was most awkward and then she asked me to tell her something about her life. I said my next available appointment is in two weeks – would you like to book an appointment? (From that moment on, I know when my next available appointment is.)

NO JUDGMENT FOR FELLOW MEDIUMS

Passing judgment on other mediums, or their style of communication from Spirit, brings your energy down. Spirit will let you know that they do not appreciate the judgment you placed. Different people are different. Get your curiosity flowing and get off the judgment train. You made mistakes and perfect does not exist unless you're Spirit.

This has happened more times than not. There are a group of friends who are doing a medium exercise of sitting in a circle. Before the start of the meditation, the conversation drives to negative talk about a fellow medium whose message was off and what she could have done or that she was not good at all. The energy of the whole room tanked. Do you expect your favorite baseball player to hit a home run every time? We are doing our best.

EVER HELPING

I walked out of the elevator and I saw a person sitting in a wheelchair struggling to get their coat on because it was stuck in some weird way that they couldn't see. Before I realized it, I hopped over to the other side of the wheelchair and pulled the coat out of the wheel behind her. Then I gently lowered the coat to ease her right arm in the jacket and then the left side. I looked at her and said, "You are all set with your cute jacket. May I open the door for you?" She said, "I'm fine. No one has ever helped me with so much love and compassion. I feel so much better about this town now. Thank you. Have a good day."

Then after she left, I realized, where did I put my purse and bag? They are twenty feet away at the elevator door because you ran like a crazy person to help her and wheel-chairs scare the shit out of you and that didn't matter. How did I help someone?

This work is sacred. This work is from Spirit. This work is about loving yourself and loving others. This work is about being of service to Spirit. Through His love, we do all things. This is not for yes or no, people. I want this gift on the weekends – I'm too busy during the week. It will take you to new thinking. It will take you away from what you call reality in the times and spaces. That is ever-changing and we can move and go with the flow and culti-vate our flow or leave it and walk away.

I went back and forth. This was not the job for me? How am I supposed to help? If you want it, there is time, effort, energy, and your loved ones involved. You have to be made of courage and strength to do daily workings with Spirit.

THE ONE WITH FORWARDING SPIRIT'S LOVE

"The greatest achievement to any human being is to love God, yourself, and others."

— JANET JACKSON

The understanding of communicating with Spirit is ongoing, ever updating and ever expanding your imagination with experiences. I'm so proud of the way you have processed all this information as it pushes your mind, body, and spirit.

I'm glad you took the time to be curious and not give into fear when all the communications were happening to you throughout your life. Sometimes a butterfly landing on a dog's nose is a sign of communication. One for sure way of knowing is if you feel the love. Cultivating that love with Spirit is exciting and you have all the laws that govern it to guide you – Law of Vibration, Natural Law, and the Laws of Mediumship.

Taking time every day to meditate and feed that communication relationship with Spirit is a sure-fire way to keep messages flowing. I think of that like a river. Sometimes you just need to look at the river and see how fast it moves. Then you want to touch the water because it looks so refreshing. Sometimes you want proof of the river to share with friends so they can be happy. The river, like communicating with Spirit, takes a lot of respect and nurturing.

Together we walked through all the keys to your foundation of how you communicate with Spirit: how your heart is most comfortable communicating with Spirit; daily meditations and why concentration is key for all of this to come together. You have a better understanding of reading energy. What is in my environment? Take notes to expand illogical experiences and understand them in a better capacity. Use logic to deepen the messages of love from spirit.

A medium is one that uses the mind to give intentions that will be carried on the law of vibration, natural law, and laws of mediumship. Understand your type of medium gifts, and how the keys collect data for our messages. After we understood how your gifts work, we explored how to use your gifts and when not to use your gifts. The medium meditates daily and is ready to communicate with Spirit to help yourself so you may help others.

You understand the consequences: what not keeping up your routine with Spirit communication can do to your mind, body, and soul health. The messages will not be clear and frustration will be present.

You activated the Seven Spirit Communication Keys for building your bond with Spirit.

The Seven Spirit Communication Keys

1. Key | Spirit's Love
2. Key | Intention
3. Key | Logic
4. Key | Dream
5. Key | Life Stories
6. Key | Psychic
7. Key | Be in the Love

Most importantly, you will have fun creating a language that is your own and personal. We walked through boundaries that need to be set with Spirit. Concentration is so important, so no matter what the message from Spirit is, you are able to understand it completely. Understand that human beings have the ability to have free will. Spirit does not dictate your life. Healthy boundaries, healthy body, mind, and soul leads to healthy communication with Spirit and your life.

LAST TRIP

After Gram passed, I moved to California and found a wonderful mental health therapist to help with grief. James was my first mental health therapist in California and he was fantastic. As he was helping me navigate through my grief, I was not feeling connected to Spirit at all. It didn't make sense to me. I had all these dreams from Spirit and Grandpa Bill. I should feel close but I don't. I stopped praying because I was not able to face my reality or put together how my life's rhythm was to be. She was gone and I had anger.

After several months had passed, I explained to James that I was sad that my Gram would never get to visit me in California and see my life. We had just said goodbye to our five house guests of the last four months, and I wanted my

Gram to visit. I was happy to have the visitors but realized Gram would never be one of them. During our therapy session, James gave me an assignment to pretend to pick up Gram at the airport and drive around town and show where I live and what I am doing with my life. Journaling about it really was not helping me at the time. At my next mental health therapy appointment, I would share the experience with James.

I was ready to complete my homework assignment from therapy. I traveled with Gram around town as if she was in my car. I was speaking to her as if she was a live person. It felt good. We drove around town and picked up ice cream and headed to the beach. I was so excited when I took her to Newport Beach. I drove to the end of the peninsula and parked. The locals call this place, "The Wedge." This is where all the boats in Newport Harbor go out to sea like the famous SS Minnow from Gilligan's Island television show. The TV show's beginning credits were filmed there and most visitors love to know this trivia about California.

After I parked the car, I walked over to the dedicated benches that face the water and sat at Jack's bench. Jack must have been a special man because he has a whole bench dedicated him. I felt all this love around his name and bench. I thought, "The family must have loved Jack to have a sweet bench." Every visitor I took to the wedge would sit on Jack's bench. I had being doing this for about three years. I walked over to the bench and saw my Gram and Grandpa sitting on Jack's bench. It was a quick picture snapshot. I sat on the bench and proceeded to share my story about the wedge with Gram and now Grandpa Bill. I finished my ice cream and journaled about my experience.

The next time at therapy, I was to share the tour of California I gave to my Gram. This was to help with my grief. I explained to James everything I just shared with you. The entire day of events and places. I told James that I liked journaling on Jack's bench because it is just cozy and loving for me.

James sat back in his chair and looked me square in the eyes and said, "Bren, Jack is my father. You took your Gram to my father's bench. My family paid for our father's dedicated bench at the Wedge in Newport Beach, CA." I sat there looking back at James with my mouth on the floor. I thought he was joking with me. James was not. I took my Gram to Jack's bench. I've taken all my visitors to Jack's bench. After I processed it, I cried. This felt like a Be in the Love Key had been placed on my lap to remind me love never ends. I know Spirit and Jack orchestrated this beautiful experience for me, for my grandparents, for James, for Jack, for Jack's family, and for you.

I can't wait for your stories of your life to be revealed to you. This is not goodbye. As we chatted earlier, we are all connected by Spirit and love. I'm glad you are understanding that mediumship is a sacred calling that Spirit knew you were able to handle. You have every right to walk away from communicating with Spirit but you know how hard it felt before.

The Seven Spirit Communication Keys are now tools for your use. As we are connected in Spirit's love, it brings me joy that you will use your medium gifts to share Spirit's love forward. I've never more excited for you than now. Thank you in advance for forwarding Spirit's love. It's a Spirit blessing to Be in the Love.

ACKNOWLEDGMENTS

This is a radically inclusive acknowledgment of all the souls that have crossed my soul's path. Every moment you dedicated to loving or hating my soul has brought me to this moment right here and right now. Thank you. There are no amount of words to give back to you that would sum up my experiences with you. Know that in my time and space, I acknowledge you right now and am loving you unconditionally. Thank you for being you and being in my life. Spirit is the key blessing to *be in the love*.

ABOUT THE AUTHOR

Reverend Brenda McCrea grew up in a small town outside of Chicago, Illinois, and moved across the country to reside in California in 2000. While in Illinois, Brenda received her bachelor's degree in communications from Eastern Illinois University, Charleston, Illinois. Little did she know how important that degree would be when speaking to the dead.

Spirit's relationship with Brenda has been strong since before she was able to speak. Her grandfather, one of the first souls she encountered, would play with her in her crib as a child; despite having passed away a year before Brenda was born. Having crossed over several times herself, Brenda has a unique synergy with Spirit that allows her to connect deeply with loved ones on the other side in a powerful love filled way.

Over four decades Brenda has successfully completed numerous certification programs for mediumship, healing and energy work. Her most recent certification has been under the mentorship of Marianne Williamson completing *A Course in Miracles*.

Brenda's approach during a reading is one of compassion, guidance, and resolution. Her open-heartedness and connection to Spirit allows the messages to be conveyed with love, hope and inspiration. This compassion has been a magnetic force that has attracted clientele from every continent.

When Brenda is not speaking to Spirit or loved ones on the other side, she can be found playing with her dogs, playing video games with her husband, or traveling the world. Brenda met her husband, Sean, in grade school and has been happily married for more than twenty-four years.

ABOUT DIFFERENCE PRESS

Difference Press is the publishing arm of The Author Incubator, an Inc. 500 award-winning company that helps business owners and executives grow their brand, establish thought leadership, and get customers, clients, and highly-paid speaking opportunities, through writing and publishing books.

While traditional publishers require that you already have a large following to guarantee they make money from sales to your existing list, our approach is focused on using a book to grow your following -- even if you currently don't have a following. This is why we charge an up-front fee but never take a percentage of revenue you earn from your book.

☞ MORE THAN A COACH. MORE THAN A PUBLISHER. ✍

We work intimately and personally with each of our authors to develop a revenue-generating strategy for the book. By using a Lean Start Up style methodology, we guarantee the book's success before we even start writing. We provide all the technical support authors need with editing, design, marketing, and publishing, the emotional support you would get from a book coach to help you manage anxiety and time constrains, and we serve as a strategic thought partner engineering the book for success.

The Author Incubator has helped almost 2,000 entrepreneurs write, publish, and promote their non-fiction books. Our authors have used their books to gain international media exposure, build a brand and marketing following, get highly-paid speaking engagements, raise awareness of their product or service, and attract clients and customers.

☞ ARE YOU READY TO WRITE A BOOK? ✍

As a client, we will work with you to make sure you book gets done right and that it gets done quickly. The Author Incubator provides one-stop for strategic book consultation, author coaching to manage writer's block and anxiety, full-service professional editing, design, and self-publishing services, and book marketing and launch campaigns. We sell this as one package so our clients are not slowed down with contradictory advice. We have a 99% success rate with nearly all of our clients completing their books, publishing them, and reaching bestseller status upon launch.

☞ APPLY NOW AND BE OUR NEXT SUCCESS STORY ✍

To find out if there is a significant ROI for you to write a book, get on our calendar by completing an application at www.TheAuthorIncubator.com/apply.

OTHER BOOKS BY DIFFERENCE PRESS

Inner Genius Outer Guru: A Heart-Centered Entrepreneur's Guide to Unlimited Potential for Growth in Income and Freedom in Lifestyle without Burnout by Avadhi Dhruv

Longevity: Reinvent Yourself at Any Age by Maria L. Ellis, MBA

Leadership Parenting: Empower Your Child's Social Success by Mother Gopi Gita

The Empowered Yogi: Transcend the Chronic Pain and Anxiety Associated with Autoimmune Conditions by Maggie Heinzel-Neel

Embracing Equity: Best Practices for Developing and Keeping a Winning Multi-Racial Leadership Team by Janine Hill, Ph.D.

Weight Loss for High Achievers: Stop Self-Sabotage and Start Losing Weight by Karen King

Profitable Online Programs: A Brief Guide to Creating and Launching an Impactful Digital Course, Then Scaling Your Biz with Your Own Expert Book! by Dr. Angela E. Lauria

Kickstart Your Online Business: Create an Online Course and Start to Make Sales by Sigrun

Take Back Your Life: Find Hope and Freedom from Fibromyalgia Symptoms and Pain by Tami Stackelhouse

The $7-Trillion Shock Wave: 401K Investing Strategies with a Positive Impact in Our Shared Climate Future by Seann Stoner

Understanding the Profiles in Human Design: The Facilitator's Guide to Unleashing Potential by Robin Winn, MFT

THANK YOU!

Please visit www.MiracleMindedMedium.com for your free gift.